Art in Action

Credits

Cover: Illustration by Judy Sakaguchi.
Illustrations: 23(r), 27, 34, 44, 53(l), Barbara Hoopes.

Publisher's Photos: All photos by Rodney Jones Studios except as credited below. Coronado photo on page 75 includes works of art within the Putnam Collection at the Timken Art Gallery, San Diego, California. Key: (t) top, (c) center, (b) bottom, (l) left, (r) right.

UNIT 1: Page 1(t), Image Bank West/Lisl Dennis; 1(b), Image Bank West/Harald Sund; 3(tl), Image Bank West/Franco Fontana; 3(tr), David Muench; 3(bl), Image Bank West/ Shirakawa; 3(br), Ewing Galloway; 4(t), Michael George/Photo Researchers, Inc.; 4(b), Image Bank West/Harald Sund; 5, Image Bank West/Alvis Upitis; 6(l), 6(tr), Three Lions; 8, David Muench; 12(t), Walter Chandoha; 16(b), Image Bank West/George Obrekski; 17, George Hall/PhotoFile; 18, EPA/Scala; 19, David Krasnor/Photo Researchers, Inc.; 24, Giraudon/Art Resource; 28, Image Bank West/Jim Adair.

UNIT 2: Page 36, Don & Pat Valenti; 37(b), Tom Myers; 42, Malcolm Varon, N.Y.C.; 43, Leven Leatherbury; 46(tl), Camerique/Joel Smith; 46(tc), Camerique/Steve McCurry; 46(tr), Milt and Joan Mann/Cameramann International; 46(bl), Camerique/Mickey Gibson; 46(bc), Camerique/Willie Hill; 46(br), Camerique; 58, Yves Siza; 68(t), Werner H. Müller/Peter Arnold, Inc.; 68(b), Sandak, Inc.; 72(t), Hélène Adant; 73(tr), Camerique.

UNIT 3: Page 74, Steve Elmore; 76(t), Douglas Mazonowicz/Monkmeyer Press; 76(b), Bradley Smith/Gemini Smith, Inc.; 77(bl), Ewing Galloway; 78(l), Lee Boltin; 78(r), Malcolm S. Kirk/Peter Arnold, Inc.; 80(l), 80(r), Scala/Art Resource; 82, Bob and Ira Spring; 83, Dennis Mock/Focus West; 84(r), Magnum Photos; 86(t), Hirmer Fotoarchiv; 86(b), Scala/Art Resource; 87(l), Gerald L. French/PhotoFile; 89, Memphis Sheet Design by Cannon; 90(l), Marie Ueda/Click/Chicago; 90(r), Giraudon/Art Resource; 97(br), Leven Leatherbury; 99, Michal Heron; 103, Carmelo Guadagno; 104(l), J. Myers/H. Armstrong Roberts, Inc.; 104(tr), A. Foley/H. Armstrong Roberts, Inc.; 104(br), H. Armstrong Roberts, Inc.; 105(l), Douglas Mazonowicz/Monkmeyer Press; 105(tr), Magnum Photos; 105(br), Carmelo Guadagno.

UNIT 4: Page 109(tr), 109(bl), Leven Leatherbury; 110(t), Courtesy Buick Motor Division; 110(b), James Sugar/Black Star; 114, *Where the Sidewalk Ends*/Shel Silverstein/Harper & Row; 118(t), 118(b), United States Postal Service; 124(tr), Irving Sloan; 124(br), Tom Myers; 127(tl), 127(bl), 127(r), E.R. Degginger; 128(t), Don Beatty; 130(l), Bob Fitch/ Black Star; 130(r), Courtesy of the Architect of the Capitol; 131(r), Shelly Katz/ Black Star; 132, Henson Associates, Inc.

Art in Action

Guy Hubbard

Indiana University

Contributing Educators:

D. Sydney Brown
Lee C. Hanson
Barbara Herberholz

CORONADO PUBLISHERS

San Diego   Orlando   Dallas   Chicago

Printed in United States of America   ISBN 0-15-770050-X(4)

1 2 3 4 5 6 7 8 9 0–93 92 91 90 89 88 87

Table of Contents

Unit 1   Seeing Like an Artist   1

1   What's My Line?   2
2   In All Directions   4
3   Aardvarks to Zebras in Lines   6
4   Shapes in Nature   8
5   Lines in Hiding   10
6   How Does It Feel?   12
7   Shaping Up Your Work   14
8   A Balancing Act   16
9   Light and Dark   18
10   Coloring Pictures   20
11   Warming Up to Cool Colors   22
12   A Bright Idea   24
13   Shades and Tints   26
14   It's Important!   28
15   Pictures Have Rhythm   30
16   Using Imagination   32
      Exploring Art: Your Art Tools   34
      Review: Using What You Have Learned   35

Unit 2   Exploring with the Tools of Art   36

17   Looking at Things from All Sides   38
18   Exploring Special Places   40
19   Looking at Landscapes   42
20   Far and Near   44
21   Exploring Photography   46
22   Putting on a Happy Face   48
23   Clowning Around with Clay   50
24   Making Faces   52
25   One of a Kind   54

26 Observing People   56
27 Looking at Still Life   58
28 In Stitches   60
29 Piecing Together a Picture   62
30 Looking at Printmaking   64
31 Threads of Evidence   66
32 Exploring Buildings   68
33 Pictures from Patches   70
    Exploring Art: Focus on an Artist   72
    Review: Using What You Have Learned   73

Unit 3   Art Then and Now   74

34 Hunting for Graphics   76
35 A Treasured Mask   78
36 Under the Wire   80
37 Bridging the Gap   82
38 A Horse of a Different Color   84
39 In Pieces   86
40 Designs on Cloth   88
41 Through a Leaded Glass   90
42 Seeing the Trees Through the Forest   92
43 Making Waves   94
44 Putting Your Best Face Forward   96
45 The Nature of Their Art   98
46 Exploring Feelings in Pictures   100
47 Once Again, with Feeling   102
    Exploring Art: Costumes and Cultures   104
    Review: Using What You Have Learned   105

Unit 4   Art Enriches Our Environment   106

48 Like No One Else Can   108
49 On the Move   110
50 Picturing Books   112
51 Wordy Pictures   114
52 A Comic Idea   116

53 Putting Your Stamp on It   118
54 A Colorful Cloth   120
55 Making Stencils   122
56 Fiddling Around   124
57 Picturing Your Community   126
58 Off the Wall   128
59 Local Heroes   130
60 Making a Friend   132
    Exploring Art: Puppet Play   134
    Review: Using What You Have Learned   135

Glossary   136
Artists' Reference   142
Index   144

Unit 1

Seeing Like an Artist

Georgia O'Keeffe, Barn with Snow, 1934, Oil on canvas. San Diego Museum of Art Collection with Permission from Georgia O'Keeffe.

Look at the painting, *Barn with Snow* by Georgia O'Keeffe. How many squares can you find? How many rectangles do you see? Name three colors in the painting. Find the lines of the roofs. What other lines do you see? Find dark areas in the painting. Where do you see light areas?

Mississippi River at Nauvoo, Illinois. Lisl Dennis.

Street Scene, San Francisco. Harald Sund.

What is art? Anything that shows or tells about ideas, feelings, or experiences is art. Paintings, photographs, poems, stories, plays, songs, and dances are art. Art is like magic. Art helps you appreciate what is around you.

Where is art? Art is everywhere. It is in the trees and clouds and shadows on the sidewalk. It is in the clothes you wear, the dishes you eat from, the furniture in your home. Art is in museums and in libraries. Art is in your classroom.

Who is an artist? Anyone who wants to share with others is an artist. Artists share their feelings and ideas. Artists show or tell others about their experiences. Anyone with imagination is an artist. You are an artist.

Studying the **elements** and **principles** of art can help you understand art better. The elements are like the pieces of a puzzle. One piece means nothing when it is by itself. It is only when all the pieces are put together that the puzzle is complete.

The principles of art are the plans that make the elements come together. The principles make order. The principles organize a work of art.

Elements	Principles
·line	·balance
·shape	·unity
·texture	·emphasis
·space	·rhythm
·value	
·color	

1 What's My Line?

Observing and Thinking

A **line** is a path that a point has followed. The point of a pencil can make a line. The point of a paintbrush can make a line. Your finger in the sand can make one, too. Think of other things that can make lines.

In his painting, *The Purple Robe,* Henri Matisse made many different kinds of lines. Find thick lines and thin lines. Look for wavy and curling lines. Are there straight lines? Point out short lines and long lines.

Henri Matisse, Purple Robe and Anemones, *1937, Oil on canvas, 28¾" × 23¾". Baltimore Museum of Art: The Cone Collection, formed by Dr. Claribal Cone and Miss Etta Cone of Baltimore, Maryland. BMA 1950. 261*

Which lines did Matisse make by scratching away paint to show the white canvas underneath? Which lines did he make with the point of a paintbrush? Find the lines that show movement in the purple robe.

Does Matisse's painting seem active or restful? Jagged lines give the feeling of activity and movement. Curving lines suggest restfulness. Which kind of line did Matisse use in *The Purple Robe?*

2

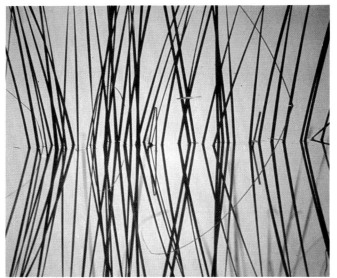

Reflected Reeds. *Franco Fontana.*

Ocotillo and Prickly Pear Cactus, *Chisos Mountains. David Muench.*

Caribou, *Alaska. Shirakawa.*

Creating Art

1. Study the lines in the above scenes from nature. Which lines are straight? Which lines are jagged? Find curving lines.

2. Look around you. Find lines in nature. Choose one thing from nature to examine closely. Then use different kinds of lines to make a drawing of that thing from nature.

Art Materials

Drawing paper   Pencil

Learning Outcomes

1. What is a line?

2. What kinds of lines did you use in your drawing?

3. Does your picture seem active or restful? Explain why.

3

2 *In All Directions*

Observing and Thinking

All lines have direction: **horizontal** —, **vertical** | , or **diagonal** /.

The picture below expresses calmness. Examine the lines in the painting. A horizontal line is at rest. It is quiet and calm.

The picture on the right suggests strength. Trace the direction of its lines. Vertical lines are strong. They are firm and give support.

The picture on the top of the next page shows movement. What kind of line does it have? Diagonal lines suggest motion and activity.

Bell Telephone Building, New York City.

Tulip Fields. *Harald Sund.*

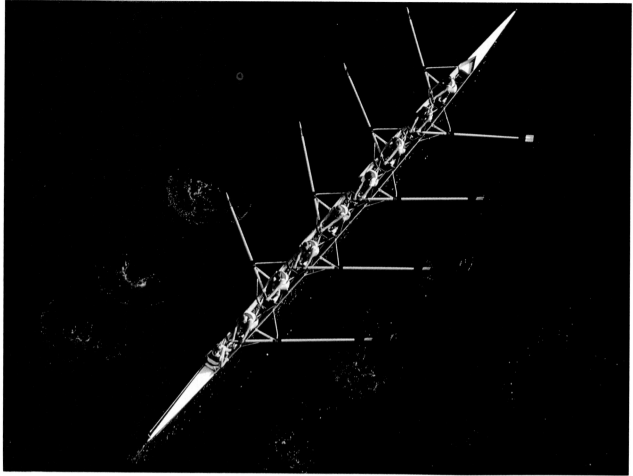

Sculling Crew, Mississippi River. *Alvis Upitis.*

Creating Art

1. Look around you. Find horizontal lines and vertical lines. Look again. Find diagonal lines.

2. Collect pictures that have diagonal lines. Study the pictures. Which lines get your attention? Do these lines move in the same direction as the edges of the picture?

3. Choose the picture from your collection that shows the most action. Make a sketch of the lines in the picture.

4. Recall the three directions lines can have. Choose one direction: horizontal, vertical, or diagonal. Draw seven lines all going the same direction.

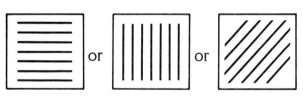

Make something out of the lines.

Art Materials	
Magazines or books with pictures	Drawing paper
	Pencil

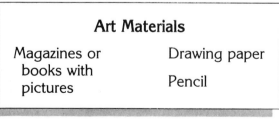

Learning Outcomes

1. What three directions can lines have?

2. What directions do the lines in your pictures have?

3. Are the lines in your drawings at rest, strong, or active? Why?

5

3 Aardvarks to Zebras in Lines

Observing and Thinking

A line that shows the edge of an object is called an **outline**. Find the outlines in these ancient cave paintings. Use your finger to trace the outlines. What animals do the outlines represent?

Long ago people lived in caves. These people made paintings of animals on the walls and ceilings of some of the caves. The artists tried to make their paintings look as real as possible.

Head of Great Bull. *Lascaux Caves, France.*

Horse. *Lascaux Caves, France.*

Look at the outlines of the animals in this ancient Japanese scroll. What animals do the outlines identify? What other things do the outlines show?

What are the animals in the scroll doing? Do animals really sit in chairs and read? When artists show animals acting like people, they are making **caricatures**.

Toba Sōjō (also known as Abbot Toba), Animal caricatures, detail of a horizontal scroll, *later Heian period, tenth to twelfth centuries, Ink on paper, approx. 12" high. National Commission for Protection of Cultural Properties of Japan, Tokyo.*

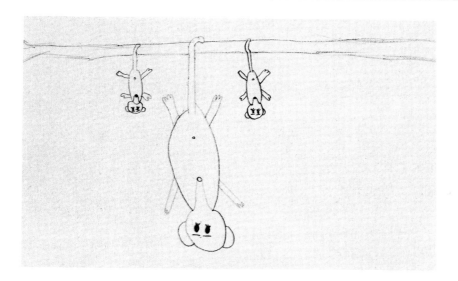

Creating Art

1. Find and study photographs of animals. Choose an animal that you would like to draw. Carefully examine that animal. Think about how it looks. Decide whether you want your animal to look real or to be a caricature.

2. Quickly sketch several outlines of your chosen subject. Examine the outlines. Decide which ones look the way you want your final drawing to be. Then on a new piece of paper, draw an outline of the animal.

Art Materials	
Drawing paper	Pencil

Learning Outcomes

1. What is an outline?

2. Of what kind of animal did you make an outline?

3. Does your outline of an animal look real or is it a caricature?

4 Shapes in Nature

Observing and Thinking

Look around you. Locate **geometric** shapes, such as circles, squares, rectangles, triangles, ovals, and ellipses. Objects that are made and used by people tend to be geometric. But nature also has geometric shapes. You can see a circle in a slice of lemon or an oval in an egg. What other natural objects can you think of that have geometric shapes?

Most shapes in nature are not geometric. They are curved and irregular. These natural shapes are countless. Examine the irregular shapes of the leaves in the photograph of a forest floor by David Muench. Trace with your finger as many shapes as you can find.

Again look around you. What shapes do you see?

Forest Floor. *David Muench.*

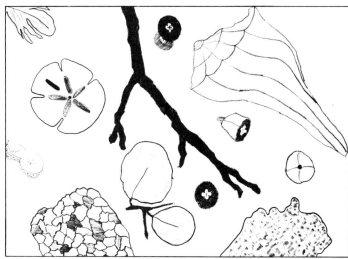

Creating Art

1. Gather a variety of objects from nature. You might choose flowers, stones, twigs, seeds, shells, nuts, and others. Choose some objects that have geometric shapes.

2. Identify the geometric and irregular shapes in your nature collection.

3. Make a sketch of some of the things in your collection. Be sure to include both irregular and geometric shapes in your drawing. Fill your whole piece of paper with shapes.

Art Materials	
Collection of objects from nature	Drawing paper
	Pencil

Learning Outcomes

1. Name three geometric shapes.

2. What kinds of shapes did you use in your drawing?

3. Which shapes in your drawing have curving lines?

9

5 Lines in Hiding

Observing and Thinking

Marc Chagall, I and the Village, 1911, Oil on canvas, 6'3⅝" × 59⅝". Collection, The Museum of Modern Art, New York, Mrs. Simon Guggenheim Fund.

Find the outlines of an animal's head and the head of a man in Marc Chagall's painting, *I and the Village.* What other lines can you see? Trace these lines with your finger.

Lines you can see are **actual lines**. Sometimes lines exist that you can't see.

Lines you cannot see are hidden or **implied lines**.

Find two circles in the painting. Notice that parts of the circles are missing. Trace the path of each circle. Let your finger complete each circle to include the implied lines.

10

Creating Art

1. Cut out three circles and two rectangles of different sizes. Lay out the shapes on a small piece of paper. Make sure the shapes overlap each other. Draw around the shapes with a pencil. Do not move or pick up the shapes until you have traced around all the shapes.

2. When you have finished tracing, remove the shapes from your paper. Look at the lines. Notice parts of the shapes are missing. Use your finger to trace the missing parts. These are the implied lines.

3. Lay out the shapes in a new way on another piece of paper. Again make sure the shapes overlap. Glue the shapes down. Find the implied lines.

Art Materials	THINK SAFETY
Construction paper	Drawing paper
	Glue
Scissors	
Pencil	

Learning Outcomes

1. What are implied lines?

2. Does your work of art have implied lines? Where?

3. Find the implied lines in the work of art on this page.

6 How Does It Feel?

Observing and Thinking

Imagine that you are holding an orange. Feel its roundness and touch its skin. Describe how its skin feels to your fingers. The way an object feels when you touch it is its **texture**. What textures do you see in the picture at the right?

Albrecht Dürer, Study of a Dog. *Trustees of the British Museum.*

Texture can be seen as well as felt. Look at Albrecht Dürer's *Study of a Dog.* Notice the way the artist used lines to show the texture of the dog's fur. Describe the texture you see. Imagine how it would feel if you could touch it.

Again look closely at *Study of a Dog.* Notice its whiskers and eyebrows. The artist was careful to add these **details**, or small parts. What other textures and details can you find in the drawing?

Creating Art

1. You can duplicate some textures around you by making a crayon rubbing. First, explore your environment to discover interesting textures. Close your eyes as you touch these textures with your fingers. Make pictures in your mind of how the textures feel.

2. Place a piece of paper over a textured surface. Use the side of a crayon with the wrapping paper removed. Rub firmly in many directions. Notice the texture as it appears on your paper.

3. You may fill another piece of paper with many different textures. You might want some textures to overlap. Use more than one color.

You can use crayon rubbings to make wrapping paper, a work folder, or a card for a friend.

Art Materials	
Drawing paper	Crayons

Learning Outcomes

1. What is texture?

2. Name the textures you made crayon rubbings of.

3. Describe the textures in the picture at the top of page 12.

7 Shaping Up Your Work

Observing and Thinking

Examine this picture. Find circles. Find ◇ shapes.

The picture above is called a **print**. Let's look at how this kind of print is made. First, an object is dipped in paint. Then it is pressed on a piece of paper. The mark left by the object is a print.

In the finished picture above, the prints are the **foreground shapes**, or first shapes. Can you find places where the print did not cover the paper? The ◇◇ are **background shapes**.

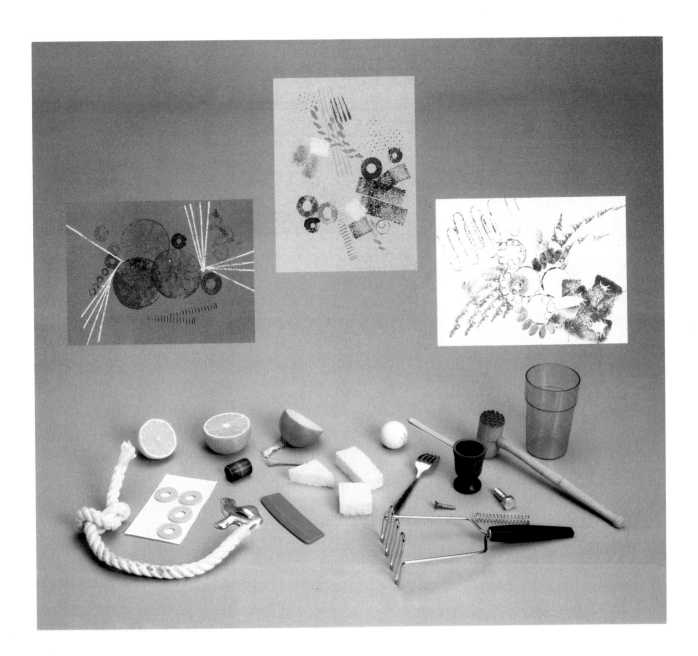

Creating Art

1. Collect several objects that you think have interesting shapes for printing. Make several practice prints with each object. First, press the object against a sponge soaked in paint. Then press the painted object on paper.

2. Examine the foreground shape left by each object. Choose which objects you want to use to make a picture. Think about the foreground and background shapes as you fill your paper with prints.

Art Materials

Found objects	Sponge on a dish
Thick tempera paint	Paper

Learning Outcomes

1. What is a foreground shape?

2. Describe how a print is made.

3. What foreground shapes are in your print?

8 A Balancing Act

Observing and Thinking

Examine the Chilkat blanket made by Tlingit Indians. For each thing on one side of the blanket, there is a similar thing on the other side. Do the things on each side of the blanket balance each other? When the two sides of a design are exactly alike, it has **symmetrical balance**. The wings of a butterfly are symmetrical.

When the two sides of a picture are very different, but are still in balance, it has **asymmetrical balance**. A teapot is asymmetrical. Find the picture with asymmetrical balance. Describe what you see. Notice that the small bicycle is balanced by the larger door.

Tlingit Indian Culture, Chief's Chilkat Blanket. *Courtesy Department Library Services, American Museum of Natural History.*

Bicycle and Wall. *George Obrekski.*

16

Look at the picture that looks like a wheel. It is a photograph of a city. A picture of a city is called a **cityscape**. Find the center of the cityscape. What shape do you see? Trace your finger along the lines or streets that move away from the center of the cityscape.

A picture that has a round center with parts that move away from it has **radial balance**. A wheel has radial balance. What other things can you think of that have radial balance?

Creating Art

1. You can make a cityscape that has balance. It can have symmetrical balance or asymmetrical balance.

2. First, use paint to make a wash for the sky in the background of your cityscape. To make a wash, use a paintbrush to spread water on a piece of paper. Add a small amount of paint. Spread the paint over the paper.

3. Think about the way you want your city to look. What kind of balance do you want it to have? Use construction paper to make the buildings in the foreground of your cityscape. Think about the shapes you want the buildings to be. You may want to draw the outlines of the buildings before you begin to cut the paper.

4. When your background wash is dry, glue on the buildings in the fore-

ground. Use felt pens, crayon, and small pieces of paper to add details.

Art Materials	⬥ THINK SAFETY
Paper	Scissors
Paint, watercolors	Pencil
Paintbrush	Felt pen
Small dish of water	Construction paper
Crayon	

Learning Outcomes

1. What kind of balance is the same on each side?

2. What kind of balance did you use in your cityscape?

3. Something in the picture at the bottom of page 16 has radial balance. Name the thing with radial balance.

17

9 *Light and Dark*

Observing and Thinking

Study this painting of a woman. Find the light areas of the painting. Find dark areas. **Value** refers to the lightness and darkness of what you see.

Why are some areas in the painting light and some dark? Light areas are being hit by light. The darker areas are not being hit by light, but are in shadow. Find the brightest light area. Find the darkest shadow. Where do you think the light is coming from?

The artist used light and dark to show the shape of the woman's face. Putting light and dark next to one another shows **contrast**, or creates differences. Find other parts of the painting where the artist used contrast.

G.A. de Predis, Portrait of Beatrice d'Este, *Formerly attributed to Leonardo da Vinci. Pinacoteca Ambrosiana, Milan.*

Walnut Grove School.

Creating Art

1. You can use a black crayon to make a drawing that shows value. You will make some areas of the drawing dark and some areas light.

   On a piece of paper, practice drawing with black crayon. Press lightly; then press hard. Make light grays, dark grays, and black. Notice the different values.

2. Think about how your school building looks on a sunny day. Think about where the sun is. What parts of the school are being hit by light? Which parts are in shadow? Make a quick sketch of how your school looks on a sunny day. Remember, areas being hit by light will be lighter than areas not being hit by light.

3. Examine your sketch. Are the light areas being hit by light? Are the dark areas in shadow? Can you tell where the light is coming from? Think about ways you can improve your sketch. Then make your final drawing.

Art Materials	
Black crayon	Drawing paper

Learning Outcomes

1. What does *value* refer to?

2. How did you show value in your picture?

3. Where is the dark area of your picture? Why is it darker there?

10 *Coloring Pictures*

Observing and Thinking

The name of a color is its **hue**. Blue, green, yellow, orange, red, and violet are hues. How many hues can you find in *The Breakfast Room* by Pierre Bonnard? Look at the color wheel at the top of the next page. Find the three **primary colors**. Red, yellow, and blue are the primary colors. If you mix yellow and red, what color will you get?

Pierre Bonnard, The Breakfast Room, c. 1930-1932, oil on canvas, 62⅞″ × 44⅞″. Collection, The Museum of Modern Art, New York, Given anonymously.

Orange is a **secondary color**. It is made by mixing two primary colors. Name the three secondary colors. Green, orange, and violet are secondary colors.

When you mix a secondary color with a primary color, you get an **intermediate** color. When you mix blue and green together, you get an intermediate color called blue-green.

How many intermediate colors can you name? Find intermediate colors in *The Breakfast Room.*

20

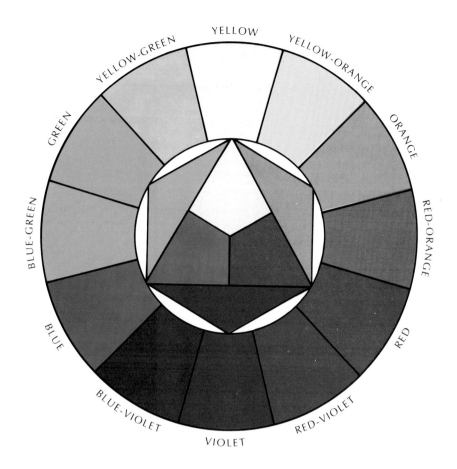

Creating Art

1. Practice the skills of using paint and a paintbrush correctly. Wash and wipe the brush when you have finished using a color, or hue. Then use the next color of paint.

2. You can mix colors with paint. First, use a white crayon to draw six overlapping circles on your paper. Paint each circle a different color. Let each circle dry before you paint another one. Use primary and secondary colors. Notice that where the circles overlap, the colors mix.

3. When you have finished see how many colors, or hues, you can find in your circles. Clean your paintbrush in water. Store it with the brush part up.

Art Materials	
Drawing paper	Paintbrush
White crayon	Small dish of water
Paint, watercolors	

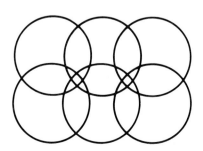

Learning Outcomes

1. What is an intermediate color?

2. What colors, or hues, did you make?

3. What intermediate colors are in the painting on page 42?

21

11 *Warming Up to Cool Colors*

Observing and Thinking

Study this color wheel. Notice that a dividing line has been drawn through yellow-green and red-violet. The colors are divided into two groups, **warm colors** and **cool colors**. Name the warm colors. Name the cool colors.

Examine the paintings on these two pages. In which painting did the artist use cool colors? The water and the colors in Claude Monet's painting give the feeling of coolness.

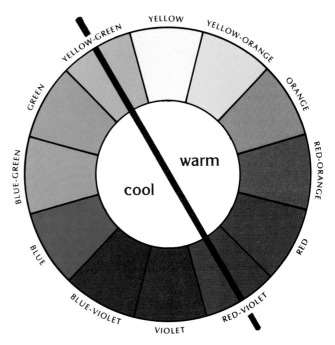

Claude Monet, Palazzo da Mula, Venice, 1908, Canvas, 24½" × 37⅞". National Gallery of Art, Washington, Chester Dale Collection.

Helen Lundeberg, Desert Coast, 1963, Oil on canvas, 60" × 60". Tobey C. Moss Gallery.

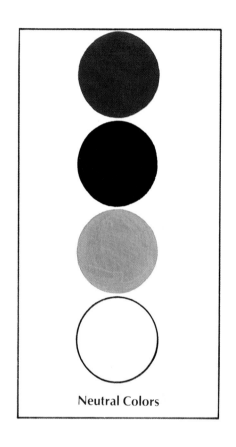

Neutral Colors

Describe a desert. Why do you think Helen Lundeberg used warm colors in her painting *Desert Coast*?

Lundeberg also used **neutral colors** in her painting. Brown, black, gray, and white are neutral colors. Find the neutral colors in *Desert Coast.*

Creating Art

1. Think of a warm or cool place. Make a picture in your mind of the place you have chosen. Think about the kinds of colors you would like the place to be. The colors you choose can be different than the place really looks. Paint a picture in your mind. If the place is cool, use cool colors. If the place is warm, use warm colors.

2. Make a crayon drawing of the place you have thought of. Use warm or cool colors. You may want to use neutral colors to add details to your drawing.

Art Materials

Crayons   Drawing paper

Learning Outcomes

1. Name the warm colors. Then name the cool colors.

2. What kinds of colors did you use in your drawing?

3. Does your picture show a feeling of coolness or of warmth? Explain why.

12 A Bright Idea

Observing and Thinking

Look at this painting by Piet Mondrian. How many lines did Mondrian use in the painting? What colors did he use? Name the geometric shapes in the painting.

Let's take a closer look at the colors Mondrian chose. Are the colors bright or dull? Are the colors **pure** or are they mixed with other colors? The **intensity** of a color is how bright or pure the color is. Mondrian chose to use intense color.

Examine the intensity of the colors around you. Find bright colors. Then find dull colors.

Piet Mondrian, Composition with Red, Blue, and Yellow, *1930. Private Collection, Zurich.*

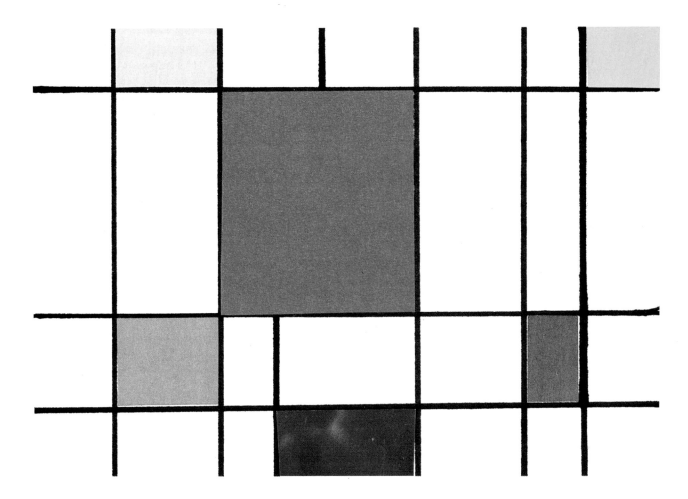

Creating Art

1. You can make a picture that uses lines, colors, and shapes in the same way that Mondrian used them in many of his paintings.

   Use black felt pen to draw five vertical lines on a piece of white paper. The lines should go all the way to the edges of the paper. Draw three horizontal lines that go to the edges of the paper. Then draw two vertical lines that stop at horizontal lines.

2. Next look through a magazine for the brightest colors you can find. Find other bright pieces of paper. Cut out these bright colors.

3. Use the bright colors you found to fill in several of the rectangles and squares made by your lines. Cut the bright colors to fit the shapes made by the lines. Arrange the colors so your work has asymmetrical balance.

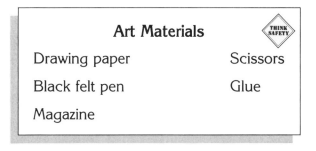

Art Materials	
Drawing paper	Scissors
Black felt pen	Glue
Magazine	

THINK SAFETY

Learning Outcomes

1. What is the intensity of a color?

2. What bright colors did you use in your work of art?

3. Name the bright colors in the picture on this page.

13 Shades and Tints

Observing and Thinking

How many different shades of green can you see in this painting? Find dark green. Find light green. The artist changed the **value** of the colors, or made them dark and light.

The artist, Toulouse-Lautrec, mixed paints to make the colors darker and lighter. The artist made **shades**, or darker colors, by adding black to green. He put some green paint on his **palette**, or mix-ing board, then added a small amount of black paint. Then he mixed the two colors together. To make even darker green he added a little more black paint.

Toulouse-Lautrec also made **tints**, or lighter colors, by adding green to white. The artist put some white paint on his pal-ette, then added drops of green paint to make light green. He added less green paint to make an even lighter green.

Henri de Toulouse-Lautrec, A Corner of the Moulin de la Galette, 1892, Cardboard mounted on wood, 39½" × 35⅛". National Gallery of Art, Washington, Chester Dale Collection.

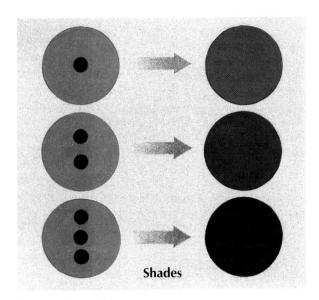

Shades

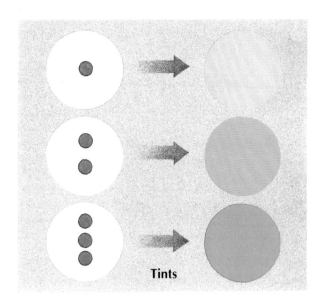

Tints

Creating Art

1. Practice mixing tints and shades on a mixing tray, or palette. Mix drops of black paint with a primary color to make shades. Then mix drops of the primary color with white paint to make tints. Remember to wash and wipe your paintbrush before you use a new color. Next make tints and shades with secondary and intermediate colors.

2. Practice using your paints and paintbrush in different ways. Make long strokes on paper. Make short strokes. Try to make a rough texture with your paint. Make thick and thin lines.

3. On a new piece of paper, you can make a painting that shows changes in value. Make tints and shades. Choose one color, or hue, to work with.

   Use the pure hue, or unmixed color, to paint a picture of an object. You can add details later.

4. Next mix some of your chosen color with two drops of black paint to make a shade. In your mind, picture a light shining down from the upper left-hand corner of your painting. Imagine what the shadow would look like. Use the mixed shade to paint the shadow.

5. Then make a tint of your chosen color by mixing two drops of the color with white paint. Use this tint to paint the background.

   Make a very dark shade of the color by mixing the color with three drops of black paint. Use this dark shade to add details to your painting.

Art Materials	
Tempera paint	Mixing tray
Paintbrush	Paper
Small dish of water	Paper towel

Learning Outcomes

1. What is a tint? What is a shade?

2. What colors did you mix to make a tint in your painting? What colors did you use to make shades?

3. Where are the tints in the painting by Toulouse-Lautrec? Find the shades.

14 It's Important!

Observing and Thinking

Look at the photograph below. What is the first thing you see? The photographer wanted to make the child in the raincoat the most important thing in the picture. When an artist makes part of a picture more important than another, it is called **emphasis**.

Emphasis gets your attention. Artists can show emphasis in many different ways. Let's look closer at the photograph to see how this artist showed emphasis. First, use your thumb to cover up the child in the raincoat. What colors do you see? Now take your thumb off the child. What colors do you see now? What did the photographer use to show emphasis in his picture?

Boy in Orange Slicker on Green Bench. *Jim Adair*.

Color is not the only way the artist showed emphasis in his work of art. Find the lines that are made by the boards in the bench. Where do these lines point? What is the second way the photographer used to show emphasis?

Color and line are two ways an artist can show emphasis.

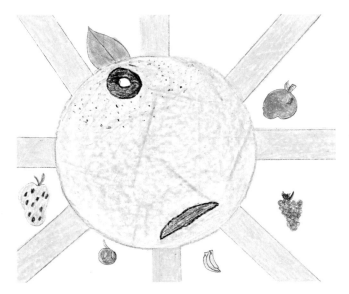

What are the most important parts of these pictures? How did the artists show emphasis in their pictures? Size is another way artists show emphasis

Creating Art

1. Think of the foods you like to eat. What shapes do the foods have? What textures are they? Then think of the food you like best of all. What color is it? What kinds of lines could you use to draw your favorite food.

2. Then draw a picture of the foods you like to eat. Make your favorite food the most important part of the picture. You can use size or the elements of color and line to put emphasis on your favorite food.

Art Materials	
Drawing paper	Crayons

Learning Outcomes

1. What is it called when an artist makes part of a picture more important than another?

2. What is the most important part of your picture?

3. What is the most important part of the picture at the bottom of page 118? How did the artist show emphasis?

29

15 *Pictures Have Rhythm*

Observing and Thinking

How would you describe the shapes that are repeated in the painting by Charles Sheeler? What kinds of lines are repeated throughout the painting?

Repetition in an artwork makes all the parts come together. When the parts of a work come together, the work has **unity**. Each part fits with the others.

Charles Sheeler, Pertaining to Yachts and Yachting, *1922, oil on canvas, 20" × 24".*
Philadelphia Museum of Art: Bequest of Margaretta S. Hinchman.

Think of a song you've heard that has a beat. The beat is repeated. The song has **rhythm**. When parts of a painting or other work of art are repeated, the work has rhythm. Does Charles Sheeler's painting have rhythm? Explain why.

Do any of the shapes in the painting **overlap**, or lie on top of, one another? Overlapping makes the parts on top look closer. Which boats look closest to you?

30

Look at the work of art made by a student artist. What shapes are repeated in it? Does the picture have rhythm? Explain why. Do all the parts of the painting seem to fit together? Why?

Which boats look closer than others? How did the artist make some boats look closer than others?

Creating Art

1. You can use triangles cut out of tissue paper to make a picture of a sailboat race. You can use repetition to make your picture have rhythm. Cut several large triangles out of a variety of colors of tissue paper.

2. Use a paintbrush to spread starch or very thin white glue on a piece of drawing paper. Overlap your tissue paper triangles on the paper. Put a small amount of starch or very thin glue over each triangle. You might want to add details with paint.

Art Materials	THINK SAFETY
Tissue paper	Paintbrush
Starch or very thin white glue	Drawing paper

Learning Outcomes

1. What makes a picture have rhythm?

2. What shapes did you repeat in your picture of a sailboat race?

3. Does your picture have rhythm? Explain why.

16 Using Imagination

Observing and Thinking

What do you see?

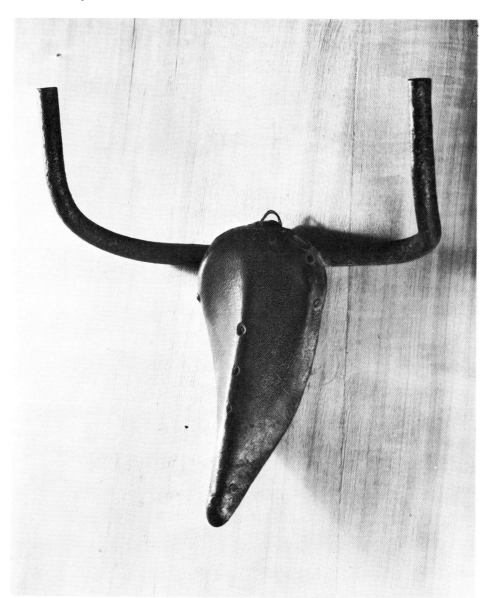

Pablo Picasso, Bull's Head, *1943, handlebars and seat of a bicycle. © S.P.A.D.E.M., Paris/V.A.G.A., New York, 1985.*

Is this a bicycle seat and handlebars? Or is it a bull's head?

Imagination is seeing something in a new way. An artist uses imagination to make a work of art.

A famous artist, Pablo Picasso, used his imagination to make this sculpture. He found a bicycle seat and a set of handlebars. Then he put the objects together in a new way.

32

Creating Art

1. Use your imagination. Collect many different kinds of objects. Then put the objects together in new ways. Use the things in your collection to make faces, animals, and new kinds of cars. What other things can you make from your found objects? Try using each object in more than one way.

2. Finally, make a found-objects sculpture. Put some of the things in your collection together in a new way. You may want to use glue, thread, or nails to make the parts of your sculpture stay together.

Art Materials	THINK SAFETY
Glue, needle and thread, or hammer and nails	Found objects

Learning Outcomes

1. What is imagination?

2. What objects did you use to make your sculpture?

3. What did you make with your imagination and your found objects?

Exploring Art

Your Art Tools

Think about the materials and tools you have used in this unit. Think about how nice it is to use these tools when they are clean and like new. You can keep these tools in good condition by taking care of them. Always clean your tools and work area when you have finished working. Learn how to store your tools and materials properly.

Work with your teacher and classmates to set up standards for taking care of your tools and materials. Make posters that show the best ways to care for your art supplies and equipment.

Enjoy the beauty of the tools you use.

Review

Using What You Have Learned

I and the Village was painted by Marc Chagall, a Russian artist. Chagall's works are imaginative and dreamlike. *I and the Village* shows the Russian village in which Chagall grew up. Notice the upside-down buildings and people in the painting. Upside-down figures and bright colors are parts of many of his paintings.

Marc Chagall, I and the Village, 1911, Oil on canvas, 6'3⅝" × 59⅝". Collection, The Museum of Modern Art, New York, Mrs. Simon Guggenheim Fund.

1. Find three diagonal lines in *I and the Village.* Find two implied lines.
2. Identify two objects that are created by outlines. What geometric shapes are in the picture?
3. Name the primary colors in Marc Chagall's painting. What secondary colors, or hues, do you see? Find two intermediate colors.
4. Find tints and shades of red and blue. Where did the artist show contrast?
5. What kind of balance does the artwork have? How did the artist show emphasis in *I and the Village?*

35

Unit 2

Exploring with the Tools of Art

What is the man in this picture doing? What materials and equipment is he using? Why do you think he chose to work where he is? Compare his painting to the place where he is looking.

Artists work in many different ways and for many different reasons. Some artists work inside; some work outside. Some create works of art only for the fun of it; others create works of art as their jobs.

Some artists paint; other artists work with clay. Some artists take photographs; others use a needle and thread. What kinds of materials, or media, are the artists in these pictures working with?

Painters, sculptors, photographers, and other artists work in a variety of places. Many artists have a special kind of workplace called a **studio**. The studio might be a room in a building or it might be an entire building. In the studio, the artist has all of his or her equipment and materials within reach. Which artist is working in a studio? What special equipment and tools are nearby to help the artist?

Most artists, even if they have studios, also work in other places. Artists go *on location* to see what things are like in different places. If an artist wants to make a drawing of a mountain, that artist might go to that mountain to make the work of art. By going on location, the artist can carefully observe the mountain as he or she draws it. Which artist is working on location? Why do you think an artist would want to work on location?

Some artists create works of art as their careers. They sell their artworks to people and to companies who use them. Some artists created and sold artworks to help make this book. Artists create posters, advertisements, and pictures in books. What other things do artists create as part of their jobs?

17 Looking at Things from All Sides

Observing and Thinking

Works of art can be separated into two groups: many-sided and flat. Many-sided objects are **three-dimensional**. A shoe is three-dimensional. It has a top, a bottom, a front, a back, a left side, and a right side. You can touch and see these sides. It has many **viewpoints**. If you put a shoe on a table you can move around the table to see different views of the shoe.

Most flat objects are **two-dimensional**. A painting is two-dimensional. It has only one side that shows a picture. If you turn a painting over, the back is blank. If you put a painting on a table and walk around the table, you do not see anything new. Look around your classroom. Find a two-dimensional object.

A sculpture, like *Bull's Head* by Picasso on page 32, is three-dimensional. It has many sides. It can be seen from many viewpoints.

Drawings, paintings, and photographs are two-dimensional. Pictures are usually on only one side of them. They are flat.

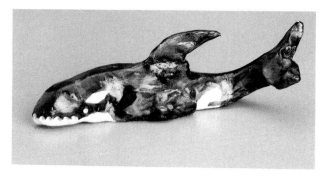

Creating Art

1. You can make a two-dimensional drawing of a three-dimensional object, such as a shoe. Examine the object carefully from all sides.

   What textures does it have? What is its shape? What kinds of lines does it have? What colors is it? Does it have tints and shades or is it evenly colored? Notice the details.

2. Make some quick pencil sketches of the object. Choose a different viewpoint for each sketch. Then on a new piece of paper, make your final crayon drawing. Include texture, line, color, and shape. Be sure to add details.

Art Materials

Drawing paper   Crayons

Pencil

Learning Outcomes

1. What is the difference between two-dimensional objects and three-dimensional objects?

2. From which viewpoint did you make your drawing: top, bottom, front, back, left side, or right side?

3. Find a two-dimensional work of art and a three-dimensional work of art in this book.

18 *Exploring Special Places*

Observing and Thinking

Think of your favorite place outdoors. Imagine that you are sitting in the middle of this place. Hear the sounds. See the shapes. A view of outdoor scenery, such as mountains, rivers, fields, or forests, is called a **landscape**.

Look at the landscape below. *Winter Landscape* is an **ink** drawing by the Japanese artist Sesshū.

Examine the lines. Notice how the lines make shapes. Find triangles and rectangles. Trace with your finger the irregular outlines of the mountains and trees.

Artists use many different materials, or **media**, to express themselves. Ink is one kind of material, or **medium**. Sesshū used ink on paper to illustrate this special place in Japan.

Sesshū, Winter Landscape, *Ink. Tokyo National Museum, Tokyo, Japan.*

Creating Art

1. Again imagine yourself sitting in the middle of your favorite place outdoors. Think about the shapes of the natural objects around you. Picture the outlines of the large objects around you. Look closer and see the textures that nature has created.

2. Use pen to make some quick sketches of the things you have imagined around you. Practice making outlines. Try different ways to show the shapes and textures. Use different kinds of pens to see the various lines and marks they make. Keep thinking about your favorite place outside.

3. Study the shapes, lines, and textures of your sketches. Decide which parts best show what your favorite place outside is like. Use these shapes, lines, and textures to make an ink drawing of your favorite landscape.

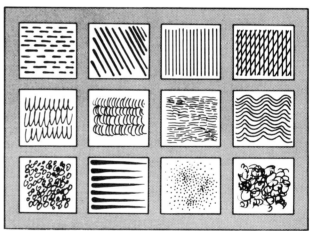

Art Materials

Drawing paper   Pens

Learning Outcomes

1. What is a landscape?

2. What medium did you use to make your landscape drawing?

3. Find shapes, lines, and textures in the landscape drawing on this page.

19 Looking at Landscapes

Observing and Thinking

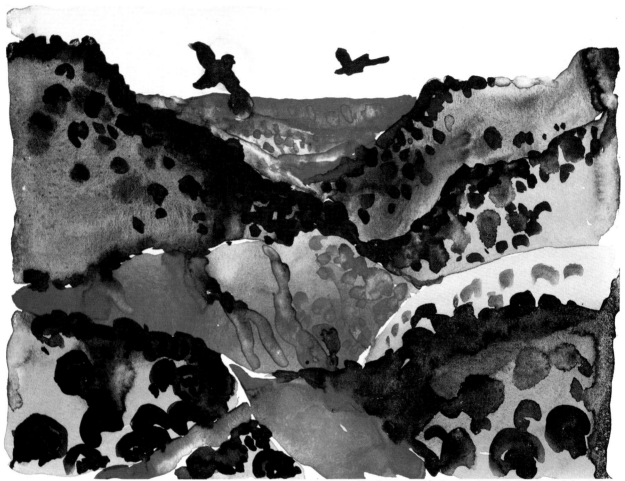

Georgia O'Keeffe, Canyon with Crows, 1917. *Collection of the Artist.*

Watercolor is a medium used by many painters. Watercolor is a **transparent** paint, which means you can see through the paint. Notice that in many parts of *Canyon with Crows* you can see the paper beneath the paint. Find areas where you can see colors of paint underneath other colors of paint.

Study the value of colors in the landscape painting by Georgia O'Keeffe.

Which paint did she put down first, the light colors or the dark colors? Find areas where black was painted over other colors. With watercolors, dark colors can go over light, but light colors cannot go over dark. When painting dark colors over light, the light colors must dry first.

Creating Art

1. Practice painting the sky by making a wash on wet paper. Use a wet paintbrush to moisten the paper. While the paper is wet, add blue paint. Spread the paint across the paper.

2. On another piece of paper, practice painting mountains by making a wash on dry paper. Make the outline of the mountains with paint on dry paper. Then dampen the brush and pull the color of the outline down to make a wash. Notice that the mountains are darker near the outline.

3. Use a new piece of paper to practice different kinds of strokes to create trees and bushes. Pull, press, roll, and make dots with the brush and paint. Explore using a dry paintbrush. After filling it with paint, wipe the brush on a paper towel. Then make textured strokes on your paper.

4. Spread a dark color of paint on half a piece of paper. Clean your brush in your dish of water. Then spread a light color of paint on the other half of the paper. Let the paint dry.

   Put light paint over the dark paint. What happens? Put dark paint over the light paint. What happens?

5. Examine the techniques you have practiced. Decide which techniques you like best. Use watercolors to create a landscape painting.

Art Materials	
Paper	Paper towels
Small dish of water	Paintbrush
Watercolors	

Learning Outcomes

1. Why is watercolor a transparent paint?

2. What happens if you put a light color of watercolor over a dark color of watercolor?

3. Find textures in the watercolor painting on this page.

20 *Far and Near*

Observing and Thinking

You have probably used **crayons** since you were a small child. But did you know that famous artists, such as Leonardo da Vinci and Michelangelo, used crayons to draw pictures?

Look at this crayon landscape drawing. Which trees look closest to you? You know that artists use overlapping to show which objects are closest.

But artists can also use size to show which objects are close and which are far away. Find the smallest trees in the crayon drawing. Do these trees look close or far away?

As things get farther away, they look smaller. Artists show that objects are far away by making them smaller than the objects that are close.

Untitled crayon landscape. Collection of the artist.

Creating Art

1. Landscape drawings that show which objects are close and which are far away need to be planned. One way to do this is to make a practice sketch.

   Draw a horizontal line across the middle of your paper. The line, called the **horizon**, shows where the sky meets the ground.

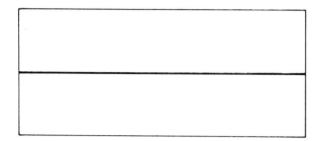

2. Starting near the bottom of your practice sketch, quickly draw three fairly large trees. The leaves of the trees can cross over the horizon line. Overlap two of the trees so that one looks a little closer than the other.

3. Next, draw four small trees between the large trees in front and the sky, or horizon line, in the back. The leaves of the trees can cross over the horizon line. By making these trees small, you make them look far away.

4. Study your sketch. Then make a crayon drawing of a landscape with trees. Last of all, fill in the sky and add details to your drawing.

Art Materials	
Drawing paper	Crayons

Learning Outcomes

1. Name two ways artists show which things are close and which things are far away.

2. How did you make some trees look farther away than others?

3. Turn to the painting on page 20. Which things are closest to you? Which things are farthest away? How do you know?

21 *Exploring Photography*

Observing and Thinking

When you smile, what are you feeling inside? What about when you frown? People have many feelings. Their faces can show these feelings.

The looks on people's faces are called **expressions**. A smile is an expression; so is a frown. How many expressions can you make your face show?

What do these pictures tell you about the people in them? What might each person be feeling inside?

A picture that tells about a person is called a **portrait**. These portraits were made by artists called **photographers**. Photographers use film and cameras to make pictures.

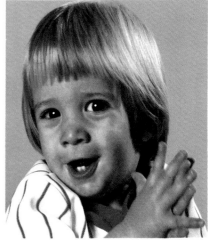

Creating Art

1. Make a collection of photographs that show expressions on the faces of people. You may find these photographs in magazines and newspapers. Or you may take the photographs yourself. Choose the portraits that have the best expressions.

2. Arrange your photograph collection on a large piece of paper. When the photographs are in balance, paste each one to the paper.

Art Materials

Magazines or film and camera	Construction paper
Glue	Scissors

Learning Outcomes

1. What is a portrait?

2. What expressions did you include in your collection?

3. Look at the portrait on page 2. What might this person be feeling inside?

47

22 *Putting on a Happy Face*

Observing and Thinking

Let's look at a kind of three-dimensional art called **sculpture**. Sculptures have many sides. You can look at them from many different viewpoints.

Eskimo Wooden Dance Mask, *representing Negafok, the Cold Weather Spirit, c. 1875, 30"' high. Courtesy of Museum of the American Indian, Heye Foundation, N.Y.*

Study the wooden mask made by an Alaskan Eskimo. Find the parts on the mask where the artist cut away pieces of the wood. **Subtractive sculpture** is made when an artist carves, or cuts away, some of the material. When you cut a pumpkin to make a jack-o'-lantern, you are making a subtractive sculpture.

Look at the mask again. What materials and objects did the artist add to the mask? **Additive sculpture** is made when an artist adds materials to the sculpture. When you made a work of art from objects you found, you made an additive sculpture.

The mask shows the spirit of cold weather and storms. Notice the sad expression on the mask. Eskimos believed that the spirit of cold weather and storms was sad because it had to leave when the warm spring weather came.

Creating Art

1. Make a three-dimensional mask out of a paper bag. Most of the mask will be an additive sculpture because you will add paper to it. Choose a paper bag large enough to fit over your head. Put the bag over your head and locate your eyes. Remove the bag and cut small openings for your eyes. The cut part of the mask is subtractive sculpture.

2. Think of the expression you want your mask to have. Then curl, bend, cut, tear, and fold pieces of colored paper to decorate your mask. Attach these pieces of paper to the bag with glue or tape.

Art Materials

Paper bag	Scissors
Colored construction paper	Glue or tape

Learning Outcomes

1. What is the difference between additive sculpture and subtractive sculpture?

2. Which kind of sculpture is your mask? Explain why.

3. Look at the sculpture on page 96. Is it additive or subtractive? Explain why.

23 Clowning Around with Clay

Observing and Thinking

Where have you seen clowns? Look at this clown called *The Jester* by Pablo Picasso. Describe the texture of the sculpture. Is this work of art two-dimensional or three-dimensional? Why do you say so?

Pablo Picasso, The Jester, 1905, Bronze, 15¾" × 13¾" × 8⅝". Collection of Mrs. Bertram Smith, New York.

Pablo Picasso made this face of a clown out of a metal called **bronze**. But bronze is too hard to cut. So first, he carved and **modeled**, or formed with his hands, a big piece of wax. Wax is very soft. It can be carved easily.

Then Picasso made a **mold** out of clay to fit around the wax sculpture. Ice-cube trays are a kind of mold. They make ice cubes into square shapes. Picasso's mold made a clown shape.

Bronze was heated to a very high temperature. It became so hot that it melted. The bronze was poured into the clown-shaped mold. When the bronze cooled, it became hard again. Picasso had made the bronze into a clown shape.

Creating Art

1. You can use clay to make a sculpture of a clown's head. Clay is soft and can be carved, or cut away. Your clown will be carved and modeled, or shaped with your hands. Think about the kind of clown you will make.

2. Roll a piece of clay into a cylinder:

3. Stand the cylinder up and pinch in near the bottom to form the neck and shoulders. Make the neck thick and the shoulders wide to hold up the head.

4. Begin modeling the head of the clown. Shape the head with your hands. Pinch the clay to form hair and a nose. Be sure to turn the sculpture so that you see all the sides as you work.

5. Use a toothpick or the handle of a spoon to carve the eyes and mouth. Carve away other details. Give the hair texture.

Art Materials	
Toothpicks or a spoon	Clay

Learning Outcomes

1. What is the difference between modeling and carving?

2. What parts did you carve in your sculpture?

3. Compare the textures in the sculptures on these two pages.

24 Making Faces

Observing and Thinking

Study the lines in this portrait by Edgar Degas. Notice how the lines show the texture of the man's curly hair and stiff beard. His face and hands are smooth. If you carefully examine the lines in the jacket, you will see that the lines themselves have texture.

Edgar Degas, Portrait of Edmond Duranty, *about 1879, Charcoal. The Metropolitan Museum of Art, Rogers Fund, 1918. (19.51.9A)*

Edgar Degas used **charcoal** to draw this portrait. Charcoal is soft. Its lines not only show texture; they have texture.

Creating Art

1. Use pencil to make a practice drawing of a person's face. First, fold your paper in half, then in half again. Open it up so it looks like this:

2. Draw an oval on the paper. Remember that an oval is egg-shaped. Leave room for the hair, ears, and neck.

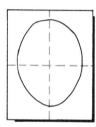

3. Draw the eyes on the fold that goes across. Draw the nose and lips on the fold that goes down. Draw the ears just below the line that goes across.

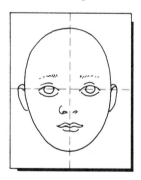

4. Last of all draw the hair and neck.

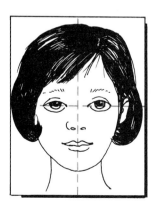

5. Now you are ready to draw a portrait in charcoal or black crayon. Study the face of the person you want to draw. Look at the shape of that person's head. Are the eyes close together or far apart? What color are they?

What is the shape of the person's nose and lips? What are the ears like? What texture is the hair?

6. After studying the person's face, follow the steps for drawing a face. Draw a portrait in charcoal or black crayon.

Below is a portrait drawn by an artist your age.

Art Materials

Drawing paper	Charcoal
Pencil	or black crayon

Learning Outcomes

1. On what line did you draw the eyes in your portrait?

2. On what line did you draw the nose and lips?

3. What kinds of lines were used in the charcoal drawing on this page?

25 One of a Kind

Observing and Thinking

Describe what you see in this picture. What details do you see?

Sir Hubert von Herkomer, Head of an Old Man, *Monoprint. The Library of Congress,* Washington, D.C.

Head of an Old Man is a print. You have made prints using found objects. The artist used a flat surface, paint, and a piece of paper to make this kind of print. It is a **monoprint** because only one print can be made of each picture.

To make a monoprint, paint is spread evenly on a flat surface. Then the design is made by scraping through the paint, like making a finger painting. Study *Head of an Old Man* to see the different kinds of lines and shapes the artist made in the paint.

Finally, before the paint dries, a piece of paper is put over the painted surface. The piece of paper picks up the picture. It is a monoprint.

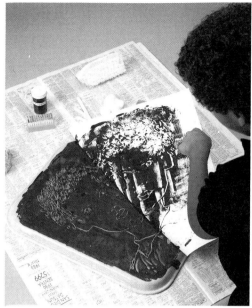

Creating Art

1. Before you make a monoprint, practice making different kinds of lines and shapes. To do this, spread paint on a flat surface, such as a tray.

   Use different objects to make lines and shapes. Try the point of a wooden stick, then the side of the stick. Use your fingers, a piece of cotton, then a piece of cloth. Try using a piece of cardboard or a comb. When you are finished practicing different lines and shapes, clean the flat surface.

2. Now you are ready to begin a monoprint. Your monoprint will be a portrait of someone you know. You can even make a **self-portrait**, a picture of yourself.

3. Spread paint on the flat surface. Create the portrait by using many different objects to make lines and shapes. Work quickly so that the paint doesn't dry too much to make a print.

4. When the portrait is finished, make a print of it by putting a piece of paper over the wet paint. Use the side of your hand to smooth the paper and press it against the paint. Then very carefully lift the paper from the painted surface.

5. Examine your monoprint. How is it different from the painted surface?

Art Materials

Tray or other flat surface	Piece of cloth
	Cardboard
Tempera paint	Comb
Wooden stick	Paper
Cotton ball	

Learning Outcomes

1. What is a monoprint?

2. How did you make different textures in your monoprint?

3. Compare the textures and lines in your monoprint and *Head of an Old Man* on page 54.

26 Observing People

Observing and Thinking

What might this man be thinking? Imagine what it would be like to be this man. What kind of work would you do? Where would you live?

An artist tries to communicate, or show, how people feel. Sometimes an artist will try to show what it is like to be someone else.

An artist must be a good observer. He or she watches people closely to learn about how they look, how they feel, and how they live.

Observe a person near you. Ask yourself, "What is it like to be that person?"

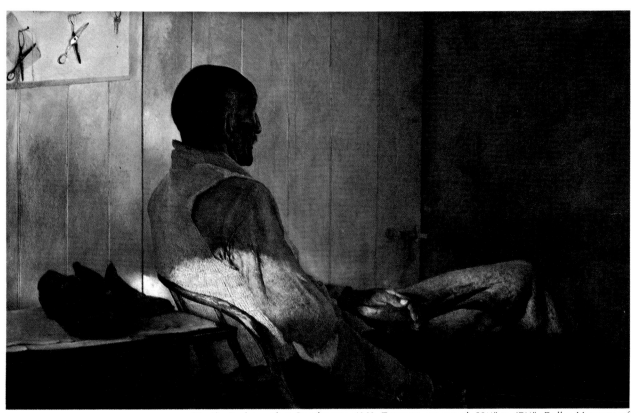

Wyeth, Andrew, That Gentleman, 1960, Tempera on panel, 23½" × 47¾". Dallas Museum of Art, Dallas Art Association Purchase.

Andrew Wyeth used **tempera** to paint this picture. Tempera is an **opaque** paint, which means you cannot see through it. With tempera, unlike with watercolors, you can put light colors over dark colors.

Creating Art

1. Use chalk to make a quick sketch of the person you will paint. First divide your paper in half, then in half again. Make an oval to match the shape of the person's head.

   Draw the shape of the person's eyes, nose, and lips. Remember to place these parts of the face on the lines.

2. Practice mixing colors to match the person's skin, eyes, and hair. Mix the colors on a mixing tray, or palette. On another piece of paper, practice making interesting textures for the skin and hair. Notice that the paint is opaque; you cannot see through it.

3. Paint the large shapes of the person's face first. When that paint has dried add details. Remember, with tempera paint you can put light colors over dark colors.

Art Materials	
Chalk	Paintbrush
Paper	Small dish of water
Mixing Tray	
Tempera paint	Paper towel

Learning Outcomes

1. Why is tempera an opaque paint?

2. What colors did you mix to make the skin, eyes, and hair of the person in your portrait?

3. What might the people in the portraits on this page be thinking?

27 *Looking at Still Life*

Observing and Thinking

Name the nonliving things you see in this picture. A picture of nonliving things is a **still life**.

What geometric shapes can you find in the still life? What irregular shapes can you find? Does the still life have symmetrical or asymmetrical balance? How do you know?

The artist used **pastels**, a kind of crayon, to make this drawing. Pastels are similar to colored chalk. If you have ever drawn on rough paper with chalk, you know that chalk shows texture. Pastels show texture on paper, too. Try to find textured areas where the pastels didn't leave color on the paper.

Jean-Etienne Liotard, French, Still Life, 1782, Pastel on parchment, 13" × 14½". Musée d'Art et d'Historie, Geneva.

How did the artist show which pieces of fruit are closest to you? Find four pieces of fruit that overlap other pieces of fruit.

Creating Art

1. You can make a still life drawing. Choose at least five non-living things to be in your picture. You will look at these real objects as you make your drawing.

   Arrange the real objects so that they have balance. Make sure that some objects are closer to you than others are. Some objects need to be behind others. That way you can overlap the things in your picture.

2. You can use pastels, crayons, or colored chalk to make your drawing. As you draw, notice the textures left by the pastel, crayon, or chalk.

Art Materials	
Pastels, crayons, or colored chalk	Drawing paper

Learning Outcomes

1. What is a still life?

2. What materials did you use to make your drawing? Compare the texture shown by these materials with the textures in the drawings on these two pages.

3. Look at the still lifes on this page. Which things look closest to you? How do you know?

28 *In Stitches*

Observing and Thinking

Some artists create pictures with a needle and thread. This kind of artwork is called **stitchery**. Examine the stitchery below. It is a kind of stitchery called **needlepoint**.

Needlepoint is made of very small stitches on a fabric screen. This still-life stitchery was made by Evangeline Greig, an American artist.

Evangeline Greig, untitled work, 1973. Collection of the artist.

Another kind of stitchery is called **embroidery**. There are many kinds of stitches used in embroidery. Look at the examples on the right.

Which kind of stitch fills in a shape? Which stitch looks like an **X**? Which stitch can make an outline?

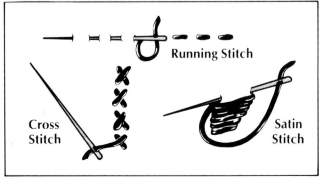

Running Stitch

Cross Stitch

Satin Stitch

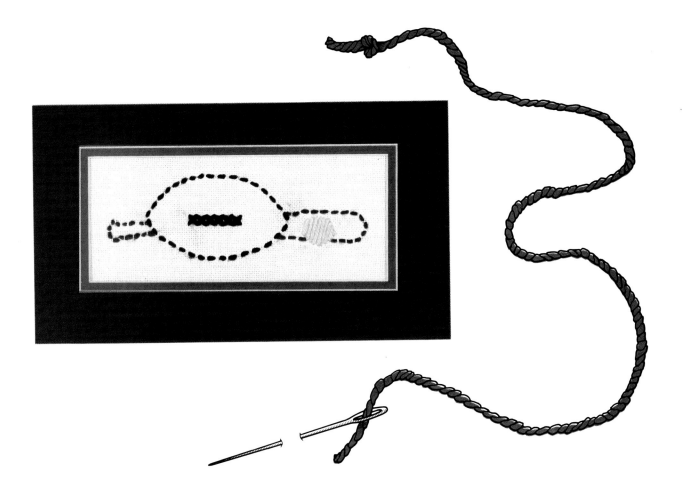

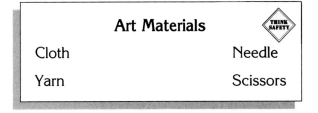

Creating Art

1. Choose three objects for a still life. It will be an embroidery. Think about the shapes and sizes of the objects. Make quick outline sketches on a piece of paper to show different ways of arranging the objects. Be sure to overlap the outlines to show which things are closest to you.

2. You need to use running stitches, satin stitches, and cross-stitches in your embroidery. Think about which things you want to be outlined with the running stitch. Which parts do you want filled in with the satin stitch? Use the cross-stitch to add details.

3. Use chalk to sketch your still life on a piece of cloth. Use a variety of colors of yarn to create your picture. Be sure to

tie a knot in the end of the yarn before you stitch.

As you work, remember that a needle is sharp. Be careful.

Art Materials	THINK SAFETY
Cloth	Needle
Yarn	Scissors

Learning Outcomes

1. Name two kinds of stitchery.

2. What stitches did you use in your stitchery?

3. Which things in your stitchery look closest to you? Explain why.

29 *Piecing Together a Picture*

Observing and Thinking

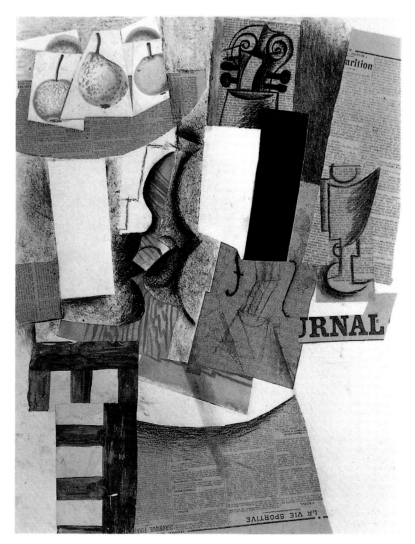

Pablo Ruiz Picasso, The Violin and Compote of Fruit, 1913, Pasted paper, charcoal, and gouache on paperboard, 25³⁄₈" × 19½". Philadelphia Museum of Art: The A.E. Gallatin Collection.

Sometimes artists find and collect the materials they will use for a work of art. Examine this picture by Pablo Picasso. What materials do you recognize? A picture that is made of collected materials is called a **collage**.

A collage has many textures and colors. You can see and feel the beauty in a collage. What textures can you find in *The Violin and Compote of Fruit*? Name the colors you see. What kinds of lines are in the picture?

In a collage, simple shapes are arranged to create an interesting design. Why does Picasso's design have unity?

Often artists make their collages look **abstract**, not the way something really looks. Does Pablo Picasso's collage look like a real violin and bowl of fruit? *The Violin and Compote of Fruit* is abstract. The violin was changed. Its parts do not look the way a violin really looks. How was the violin changed?

Creating Art

1. You can make a collage. First, collect pieces of cloth and pieces of paper. You might include wrapping paper, labels from cans, old socks, and colorful pages from magazines.

2. Examine the materials in your collection. Look for rough, smooth, thick, thin, hard, and soft pieces. Choose the materials you wish to use. Cut or tear some of the materials to change their shapes.

3. Arrange the materials on a piece of background paper. Check to see if the collage has balance. Are light colors next to dark colors for contrast? Do some of the pieces overlap others? Are some shapes large and some small?

4. When you have finished arranging the collage, attach the pieces to the background paper. Use glue, staples, or tape.

Art Materials	
Collected pieces of cloth and paper	Paper
	Glue, staples, or tape
Scissors	

Learning Outcomes

1. What is a collage?

2. What textures did you include in your collage?

3. Explain why *The Violin and Compote of Fruit* is abstract.

30 Looking at Printmaking

Observing and Thinking

Examine the picture below. It has contrasts of black and white. Find black areas. Find white areas. What shapes can you see in black? Find a sun, two birds, and four animals.

The shapes you see in black are the foreground of the picture. The white part of the picture is the background. Point to at least five places where you see white background.

Kenojuak Ashevak, The Return of the Sun, *1961. Reproduced with permission of the West Baffin Eskimo Co-operative, Cape Dorset, Northwest Territories, Canada.*

The Eskimo artist, Kenoujauk Ashevak, made this print. On a flat stone, she cut away the background. The shapes of the sun, the birds, and the animals were left. The picture you see is a print made from these shapes. It is a **relief print** because parts were carved away to leave the shapes to be printed.

Creating Art

1. You can make a print. First, think of simple shapes you know, like the outline of a duck, a candle, or a flower. Then, on a piece of paper, draw an outline of the shape you want to print.

2. Find the flat side of a potato that has been cut in half by an adult. Carefully use a nail to make the outline of your chosen shape on the flat side. The nail will carve the shape into the potato. When the shape is complete, go over it again with the nail. This time cut into the potato about ¼ of an inch.

3. Next take a spoon and carefully cut away the potato in the background. Be sure not to carve away the shape of the object to be printed.

4. Press the carved shape against a sponge soaked in thick tempera paint.

Then practice making a print on a piece of paper.

5. Finally, print a design on a new sheet of paper. Arrange the prints to make a pleasing design.

Art Materials		THINK SAFETY
Paper	Spoon	
Pencil	Thick tempera paint	
Potato		
Sponge on a dish	Nail	

Learning Outcomes

1. Find the foreground shape in your print.

2. Which part did you carve away?

3. Examine the prints at the top of the page. Find the foreground shapes. Find background shapes.

31 *Threads of Evidence*

Observing and Thinking

Long ago kings and queens and very rich people lived in palaces. The rooms of these huge buildings were cold and damp. Heavy cloths called **tapestries** were hung to help keep the palaces warm and to decorate its walls. The tapestries were rich in color and design.

Tapestries were often more than seven feet square. An ordinary tapestry took about one year to make. The best ones took up to four years. Only the very rich could afford these woven cloths.

What does this tapestry show? What kind of balance does it have?

Tapestries are a kind of **weaving**. In a weaving, threads go over and under other pieces of thread.

The Unicorn in Captivity, *detail from The Hunt of the Unicorn, VII, Tapestry. Metropolitan Museum of Art, New York.*

Look at this weaving made by a student artist. Its design does not show a picture. What colors did the artist use? Find at least two different textures in the weaving. What kind of balance does the weaving have?

Creating Art

1. You can use yarn to make a weaving that does not show a picture. First, mark the top of a piece of cardboard every ¼ inch. Then mark the bottom. Make a small cut where each mark is.

2. Next, wind string tightly around the cardboard. Tape the string down to the back of the cardboard.

3. Think about the design you want your colorful weaving to have. Choose the yarn you will use.

4. Take a piece of yarn and weave it under the first piece of string and over the second piece. It goes under and over the rest of the strings.

5. The next piece of yarn is the opposite of the first one. It will go over the first piece of string and under the second. Then it goes over and under the rest of the strings.

6. Keep the pieces of yarn close together. After weaving a piece, push it close to

the last one. Be sure to fill the space with weaving.

When you have finished your weaving, turn it over. Cut the pieces of string down the middle of the cardboard. Then tie the loose strings in knots so that the weaving will not fall apart. The fringe, or end pieces, can be trimmed.

Art Materials	THINK SAFETY
Cardboard	String
Ruler	Tape
Pencil	Yarn
Scissors	

Learning Outcomes

1. What is a tapestry?

2. Describe how the yarn and string go in a weaving.

3. What kind of balance does your weaving have?

32 *Exploring Buildings*

Observing and Thinking

Let's take a look at two buildings or pieces of **architecture**. One building is in Germany. The other is in New Mexico.

The building in Germany is a castle. Castles were built to protect people and their belongings. Notice the high wall that goes around the castle. The wall made it difficult for enemies to get inside. Find the windows. Are the windows close to the ground or up high? Why do you think the windows were put where they are?

The building in New Mexico is a mission. A mission is a kind of church. The mission is over 200 years old.

Neuschwanstein Castle. *Germany.*

Mission. *Rancho de Taos, New Mexico, 1760.*

The people who planned these buildings are called **architects**. Architects use many three-dimensional shapes, or **forms**, to design buildings. Let's look at some forms.

Again look at the two pieces of architecture. Find a cone. Find a rectangular form. Where is a cylinder?

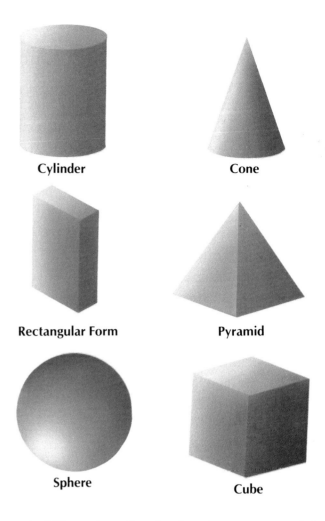

Cylinder

Cone

Rectangular Form

Pyramid

Sphere

Cube

Creating Art

1. You can use three-dimensional forms to make a plan or model of a building. You can use small boxes for cubes and rectangular forms. Paper-towel centers are cylinders. You can make paper cones.

2. Think about the kind of building you want to design. What will it be used for? Is it an office or a hotel? Will someone live or play in it?

3. Arrange the forms you might use. Do the forms have balance? Arrange the forms many times until the plan or model looks the way you want it to. Attach the forms to one another.

4. When it is finished, paint your model with tempera or spray paint.

Art Materials	THINK SAFETY
Small boxes	Construction paper
Paper-towel centers	Glue, tape, or paper clips
Tempera or spray paint	

Learning Outcomes

1. What is an architect?

2. What forms, or three-dimensional shapes, did you use in your model of a building?

3. Look at your school building. What forms does it have?

33 Pictures from Patches

Observing and Thinking

Pieces of **fabric**, or cloth, were used to make this picture of an English village. The artist cut the shapes from fabric. Then she sewed them onto a large piece of cloth to make an **appliqué**.

Richmond, England. *Private collection.*

Study the appliqué. Name the colors you see in the picture. Find three tints or shades of blue. Trace three irregular shapes with your finger. Find a smooth texture. Find a rough texture.

How many houses or parts of houses can you see? Which houses look closest to you? Which look farthest away? Where are the largest houses? Where are the smallest houses?

One way an artist can show distance is to make things smaller as they get farther away. Another way is by overlapping, or putting parts of one thing over parts of another. Find at least three houses that overlap one another.

Creating Art

1. Think of a town you have seen with many buildings. Think about the shapes of those buildings. Plan an appliqué that shows a town. It will need to have five buildings in all. Plan two large buildings and three small ones.

2. Collect pieces of fabric with many different textures and colors. Choose the shapes and colors of the buildings you would like to have in your appliqué picture. Cut the shapes of your buildings out of the pieces of fabric.

3. Arrange the five buildings on a piece of fabric or a piece of paper. Place the two large buildings on the bottom half of the picture.

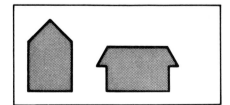

Then place the three smaller buildings in the middle of the picture. Have the larger buildings overlap the smaller ones to show distance.

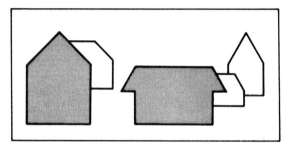

4. When you like the way the buildings are arranged, glue them down. Use small pieces of fabric to make details, such as doors, windows, chimneys, and plants.

Art Materials	
Large piece of fabric or paper	Pieces of fabric
	Glue
Scissors	

Learning Outcomes

1. What is an appliqué?

2. What textures and colors did you use in your appliqué?

3. Which buildings look closest in your appliqué? Explain why.

Exploring Art

Focus on an Artist

Henri Matisse is an artist who spent most of his life creating works of art. He was one of the most important artists of the early 1900s. He developed a style of art that was boldly simple in appearance.

Matisse worked in several different media. He created ceramics, tapestries, rugs, ballet sets, costumes, book illustrations, buildings, furniture, and stained glass, as well as paintings and drawings. He invented **découpage**, a method of creating pictures by cutting and pasting painted paper. *The Sorrow of the King* is a découpage by Matisse.

Henri Matisse, The Sorrow of the King, *1952, Photographie Musée National D'Art Moderne, Centre Georges Pompidou, Paris. All rights reserved.*

Matisse was born in France in 1869. He began to study painting in 1892. He continued to create works of art until his death in 1954.

You can choose an artist to study and write a report about. Choose an artist whose style you like or who worked in a medium you like to work in.

Review

Using What You Have Learned

Each of the three artworks on this page is a different medium. Two of the artworks are from museums: one from the British Museum in England and one from the Timken Gallery in California. Look at the **credits**, the words below the artworks, to learn more about the works of art.

Paul Cézanne, Flowers in a Glass Vase, *Putnam Foundation Collection, Timken Art Gallery, San Diego, California.*

Ife Head of a King, *Nigerian Cultures, 13th Century. Trustees of the British Museum.*

1. Look at the three artworks on this page. Which artwork is a portrait? Which is a landscape? Find the still life.

2. Look at the picture of a vase with flowers. What materials did the artist use to create this artwork?

3. Study the picture of a forest. What medium did the artist use to create this work of art? How did the artist show contrast in the artwork? Which trees are closest? How can you tell?

4. Look at the head of a man. What medium is it? How did the artist add details to the artwork?

5. Which artworks are two-dimensional? Tell why. Which are three-dimensional? Explain why.

73

Unit 3

Art Then and Now

Trinity Church and John Hancock Tower. *Copley Square Boston.*

Find the old buildings in this picture. Where do you see a new building? What do these old and new buildings tell you about the city and the people who live there?

Old art and new art both have a place in our lives. Each adds its own richness. Each has its own story to tell.

Art from the past can tell us what it was like to live long ago. It can show us how people looked, how they dressed, where they lived. Art from long ago shows what was important to the people who lived before us. Looking at old art helps us appreciate different ways of life.

We can compare the art from the past with the art that is being created today. By comparing old and new art, we can better understand the world we live in. We can see how things have changed over time. We can learn why we live as we do.

You can see art from the past in museums of art. These museums display works of art for people to look at. The museums also take care of the artworks. They protect the artworks from harm. Old works of art need special care to stop them from falling apart. Some of the people who work in museums know how to preserve works of art to make them last for many years to come.

34 Hunting for Graphics

Observing and Thinking

Yellow Horse. c. 10,000-15,000 B.C. Ceiling of the Axial Gallery, Lascaux Caves, France.

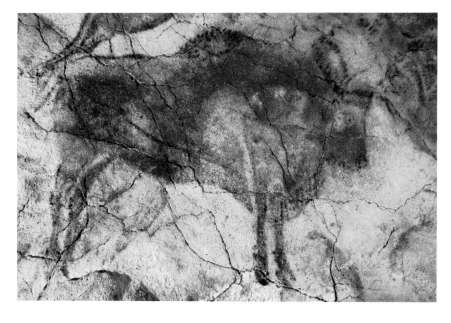

Many-colored bison. c. 12,000 B.C. Altamira Cave, Spain.

Fifteen thousand years ago people who lived in caves made drawings like these. They are outlines and simple drawings of animals that the people hunted for food. Over time we have lost the reason why the cave paintings were made. Perhaps the people believed the paintings brought them luck in the hunt. These simple drawings are messages from long ago.

Today people continue to use simple line drawings to give messages. Describe these outlines and simple pictures. What messages do they give?

Simple drawings that give a message are called **graphics**.

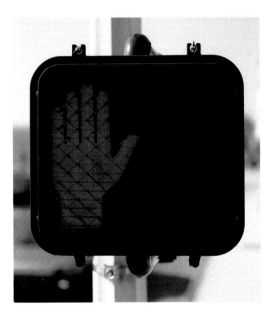

Creating Art

1. You can make a graphic for one of the following messages or a message of your own:

   - No shoes allowed.
   - Swimming is permitted.
   - Turn off the lights when you leave the room.

2. Design a graphic for a sign that gives the message that you have chosen. Be sure to keep your graphic simple. Make sketches of your ideas. Choose the one you like best. Use felt pens or crayons to create your final sign.

Art Materials	
Felt pens or crayons	Drawing paper

Learning Outcomes

1. What are graphics?

2. What shapes, lines, and colors did you use in your graphic?

3. In what ways are the cave paintings similar to today's graphics? In what ways are they different?

35 *A Treasured Mask*

Observing and Thinking

Over four thousand years ago, Egyptian kings and queens were buried in great tombs, like the three large **pyramids**. Huge treasures were buried with these royal people.

Soon thieves took the treasures from the great tombs. So the kings and queens of Egypt started hiding their tombs in the hills. Still the cunning thieves found the treasures.

Three Great Pyramids of Giza, *Egypt.*

Burial Mask of Tutankhamen, *Gold and lapis lazuli. Egyptian Museum, Cairo.*

Tutankhamen, an Egyptian king who ruled more than three thousand years ago, died when he was very young. Because he was so young, the treasure that was buried with him wasn't as large as that of older kings and queens.

When Tutankhamen's tomb was discovered in 1922, it had never been discovered by thieves. It was the largest treasure ever found in an Egyptian tomb because the others had been robbed.

Student foil mask.

Examine Tutankhamen's burial mask on page 78. It is made of gold, which is a kind of metal, and a beautiful blue stone called lapis lazuli.

Find the lines made of lapis lazuli and gold that surround the head of the mask. Notice how these lines make a frame around the young king's face. What other lines can you find in the mask? What kind of balance does the mask have?

Notice the small beard. It is a sign of royalty. It shows that this is the burial mask of a king.

Creating Art

1. You can make a mask out of a kind of metal called aluminum. The mask can be in the style of the Egyptian burial masks or any other style you choose. Plan your mask to have symmetrical balance.

2. Make a sketch on paper of the mask you plan to make. Be sure to leave some areas uncolored. Check to see that the sketch has symmetrical balance. Make any necessary changes.

3. Then on a piece of aluminum foil, use felt pens to draw your final design. Fill in any areas where you want to have color. Leave some areas uncolored so that the aluminum shows.

4. Cut out your mask. Then slightly curve the mask to make it look three-dimensional. Staple it to a piece of construction paper.

Art Materials	THINK SAFETY
Paper	Construction paper
Pencil	
Aluminum foil	Stapler
Felt pens	Scissors

Learning Outcomes

1. What is a pyramid? Why did the Egyptian kings and queens stop building pyramids?

2. What kind of balance does your aluminum mask have?

3. Compare the lines in your mask to the lines in the mask on this page.

36 Under the Wire

Observing and Thinking

About two thousand five hundred years ago, the Greeks made beautiful sculptures out of bronze, a kind of metal. Few of these sculptures have survived. Most were melted down and the metal was used again. But many of the people who melted the bronzes had them copied in **marble**, a kind of stone. So today we can see how beautiful these sculptures were.

Examine these two Greek sculptures. Which one is made of bronze? Which one is made out of marble?

Apollo Belvedere.

The *Apollo Belvedere,* shown above, is a fine example of marble sculpture. It is a copy of a Greek bronze. Describe the texture of the *Apollo Belvedere.*

Study the *Charioteer of Delphi,* the bronze sculpture on the left. Notice that the folds in the charioteer's clothes look like a column. Compare the *Charioteer of Delphi* with the *Apollo Belvedere.*

Charioteer of Delphi, c. 470 B.C., Bronze, 71" high. Delphi Museum.

Today artists still use bronze to make beautiful sculptures. Artists use other metals as well. Study this sculpture made out of metal wire. What kinds of lines does it have? Notice how the line of the wire creates the form of a person. *The Hostess* was made by Alexander Calder in 1928.

Alexander Calder, The Hostess, *1928, Wire construction, 11½" high. Collection, The Museum of Modern Art, New York. Gift of Edward M. M. Warburg.*

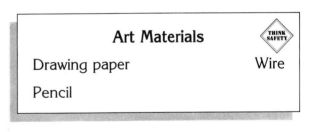

Creating Art

1. Picture yourself doing active things like playing baseball, jumping rope, or rollerskating. Picture yourself in different positions. Make several quick line drawings of yourself playing the game you chose. Decide which sketch you would like to use as a plan for a wire sculpture.

2. You may use one long piece of wire or several short pieces. Bend and twist the wire to make the shapes of your line drawing.

3. Then examine your wire sculpture. Make sure it shows action. Make changes if necessary.

Art Materials	◆ THINK SAFETY
Drawing paper	Wire
Pencil	

Learning Outcomes

1. Name two kinds of Greek sculpture.

2. Compare the lines in your wire sculpture with the lines in *The Hostess* on this page. In what ways are they different? In what ways are they the same?

3. Compare the face of the *Apollo Belvedere* with the face of *The Hostess*.

37 Bridging the Gap

Observing and Thinking

Pont du Gard. *Gard River in France.*

The Romans were excellent builders. They built this bridge almost two thousand years ago. Examine and describe the bridge. What is it made of? What kind of balance does it have? The strong bridge is still used today.

Today bridge designers go to school for many years to learn to be excellent builders. Examine and describe the bridge at the top of the next page. The modern bridge, called the Coronado Bay Bridge, goes across San Diego Bay.

Compare the Roman bridge with the Coronado Bay Bridge. Which do you think looks stronger? Why? Which is made out of stone? Which is made out of metal? Describe the shape of each bridge. Which bridge has curves? Which one has straight lines? Are both bridges useful? Why do you say so? In what ways are the bridges different? In what ways are they the same?

Coronado Bay Bridge. *San Diego, California.*

Creating Art

1. Be a bridge designer. Think about the kind of bridge you would like to make. Think about where it will be located. Will it cross a river or a bay? Or will it cross a valley? How long will it need to be? How high will it be? What kinds of lines will it have? Think about the kinds of materials you want it to be made of.

2. On a piece of paper, make several quick sketches of your ideas. Then study the sketches and decide which parts work best. On a new piece of paper, draw a plan of your bridge.

3. Finally, you can make a painting of your bridge. Choose the colors you would like it to be. Think about how you will show the textures of the materials you want the bridge to be made of. On a new piece of paper, use tem-

pera to paint the bridge. Be sure to include the river, bay, or valley that the bridge crosses.

Art Materials	
Paper	Tempera paint
Pencil	Paintbrush
Mixing tray	Small dish of water
Paper towels	

Learning Outcomes

1. Why do you think the Romans used stone to make their bridges?

2. Why do you think metal was used to make the Coronado Bay Bridge?

3. In what ways have bridges changed from Roman times to now?

38 *A Horse of a Different Color*

Observing and Thinking

Flying Horse, *Eastern Han Dynasty, 2nd century A.D., Bronze, 13½" × 17¾". People's Republic of China.*

Horse, *China, T'ang Dynasty, 618–906 A.D., Glazed terra cotta, 30¼ in. high. The Cleveland Museum of Art, Anonymous gift.*

In Chinese art the horse is a **symbol** of, or stands for, power and majesty. Emperors wanted only the best horses in their stables. They asked artists to make paintings and sculptures of their finest horses.

In China, **potters** made many clay figures of people and animals. Look at the **ceramic**, or clay, horse on the left. It was made over one thousand years ago. The potter used many colors of **glaze**, or glassy coating. The ceramic horse was **fired**, or baked, in a **kiln**, or very hot oven.

The horse on the right was made nearly two thousand years ago. It is made from bronze. Although the horse is trotting, it looks like it is flying. Notice that one hoof is placed on the back of a flying bird.

Compare the textures of the two horses. Examine the horses' heads. Which horse looks more realistic? Examine the forms of both animals. Compare the curves of the animals. Which horse looks stiff? Which horse has more curves? In sculpture, curves help show movement.

Creating Art

1. You can make a sculptured horse or other animal out of clay. First, decide which kind of animal you would like to create. Then think about the form you want your animal to have.

2. Pinch, roll, bend, and shape the clay into the form of the animal you have chosen. Be sure to look at your sculpture from all sides as you work. You can carve texture and details into your sculpture with toothpicks and other objects.

Art Materials	
Clay	Toothpicks

Learning Outcomes

1. What is the horse a symbol of in Chinese art?

2. What textures does your animal sculpture have?

3. Which horse on page 84 shows the most movement? Explain why.

85

39 In Pieces

Observing and Thinking

Let's find out about some of the ancient buildings of eastern Europe and the pictures that decorated their walls.

Find the **dome,** or half sphere, that rests on top of square walls in the Santa Sophia below. The Santa Sophia was begun in 532, nearly fifteen hundred years ago. It took five years to build. Its many windows made the inside bright. Inside, its walls are decorated with **mosaics**, pictures made with tiny pieces of colored tile or stones.

Look at the mosaics in another eastern European building, San Vitale, in Ravenna, Italy. Notice the tiny colored tiles. How many different colors can you find in the tiles? What figures do the tiles create?

Santa Sophia, *Istanbul, Turkey.*

Detail of Mosaics from the Sanctuary of San Vitale, Ravenna, A.D. 526–47.

Today we still use mosaics to decorate the walls and sometimes the floors of our buildings. Examine the modern mosaic on the left. Find the background spaces between the tiles. Describe the scene created by the tiny tiles. Compare this modern mosaic with the ancient mosaic. In what ways are they different? In what ways are they the same?

Creating Art

1. You can use colored paper to make a kind of mosaic. Think about the picture or design you want to create. Think about its shape and balance. Then cut a piece of background paper to be the size of your finished mosaic. Make a light sketch of the picture or design on your piece of background paper.

2. Cut colored paper into tiny pieces. You can use colored construction paper or colored magazine pictures. Sort the pieces by color. Keep all the red pieces together, all the blue pieces together, and so on.

3. Put paste on the backs of the tiny pieces of colored paper as you arrange them on the background. Be sure to leave very little space between the pieces of colored paper. Complete the picture or design.

Art Materials	THINK SAFETY
Piece of background paper	Colored construction paper or magazine pictures
Scissors	
Paste	

Learning Outcomes

1. What is a mosaic?

2. What kind of balance does your mosaic have?

3. Compare your mosaic with either the modern mosaic or the 1500-year-old mosaic. In what ways are they alike? How are they different?

40 Designs on Cloth

Observing and Thinking

Inca Poncho with Geometric Design. *Courtesy Department Library Services, American Museum of Natural History. #2255*

About five hundred years ago, the Inca Indians of South America had a strong empire. The Inca were skilled engineers and artists. They built roads and huge buildings. They were skilled metalworkers. Many of their gold and silver pieces still exist.

The Inca were also skilled weavers. They created beautiful **textiles**, or pieces of cloth. Examine this Inca textile. How many geometric shapes can you find? Name them. What colors are in the piece of fabric? Does the design have rhythm? Explain why.

Notice that the entire design is made of squares. Study the **patterns** created by the repetition of shapes inside the squares. Find a pattern made by repeated triangles. Find a pattern created by repeated squares.

Today we still use geometric shapes in our textiles. Think of some uses for a geometric textile. Look at this piece of cloth made by a modern designer. How many geometric shapes can you find?

Compare this modern textile with the Inca textile on page 88. In what ways are they alike? How are they different?

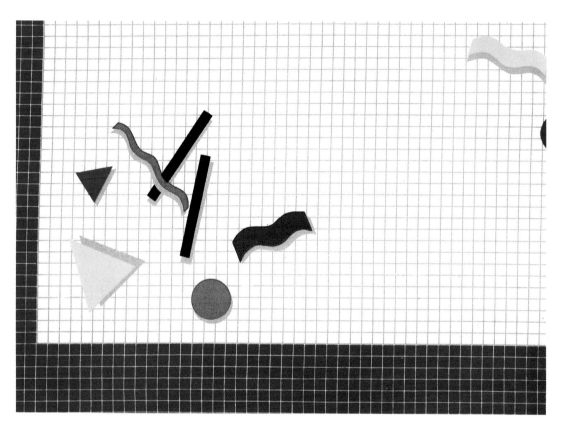

Creating Art

1. Plan a geometric design that is similar to the geometric designs in Inca textiles. You will make your design on a piece of graph paper. Use repetition to make your design have rhythm. Think about the pattern your geometric shapes will make. Choose warm or cool colors.

2. Use crayons or felt pens to make your design on the graph paper. You may want to use a ruler to make your lines very straight.

Art Materials

Graph paper   Crayons or felt pens

Ruler

Learning Outcomes

1. What is a textile?

2. What geometric shapes did you use in your graph-paper design?

3. In what ways are your design, the Inca design, and the modern-textile design the same? How are they different?

41 Through a Leaded Glass

Observing and Thinking

In the Middle Ages, huge churches were built with high ceilings and many windows. These windows were made of **stained glass**, or colored pieces of glass.

The pieces of stained glass are held together with strips of **lead**, which is a kind of metal. When light shines through the windows, the stained glass sparkles in bright colors. Light can't shine through the lead. So the strips of lead look black against the bright colors.

Examine the rose window from the Cathedral of Notre Dame in Paris, France. Look for areas of stained glass. What colors do you see? Where do you see lead? Use your finger to trace some of the black lines where light won't shine through the lead.

(below): Cathedral of Notre Dame. *Paris, France.* (right): *Rose window from south wall of the Cathedral of Notre Dame, Paris.*

What shape is the window? Notice that lines move away from the center of the circle. What kind of balance does the rose window have?

Creating Art

1. You can use construction paper and tissue paper to make a design that looks like a rose window. First, cut pieces of colored tissue paper into one-inch squares. Be sure to use many different colors.

2. Next, cut a very large circle out of black construction paper. Then fold the circle in half, then in half again, and in half one more time.

3. Along the folds in your black circle, make cuts of different shapes and sizes. Cut off the pointy tip.

4. Open up your circle and put it on a piece of wax paper. Then use a paintbrush to spread starch or very thin white glue over the design. Arrange the squares of tissue paper over the design. Make sure each cutout area is covered by tissue. You can use more than one piece of tissue to cover a cutout area.

   Then put a thin coat of starch or thin glue over the entire design.

5. Let your design dry. Then turn it over to see the many colors against the black. You can hang your design in a window or a place with a lot of light.

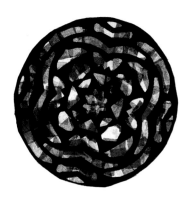

Art Materials		THINK SAFETY
Tissue paper	Starch or very thin white glue	
Scissors		
Black construction paper	Paintbrush	
	Wax paper	

Learning Outcomes

1. What is stained glass?

2. What parts of your work of art take the place of the colored glass? What part takes the place of the lead?

3. What kind of balance does your stained glass have? Explain why.

42 Seeing the Trees Through the Forest

Observing and Thinking

About five hundred years ago an artist named Leonardo da Vinci was working in Italy. He had many special talents. He was a painter, a sculptor, a scientist, and a designer of buildings. He was a great observer. He looked very closely at things to see many details. Leonardo made many sketches of things he saw. He wrote down many notes.

Let's look at one of the sketches made by Leonardo da Vinci. Notice the texture in the trunk of the tree. Find bumps in the bark on the trunk.

Examine the lines of the tree. Look for thick lines and thin lines. Look for straight lines and curved lines. Study the leaves. What kinds of lines did the artist use to make them?

Leonardo da Vinci, Study of a Tree. Royal Library, Windsor Castle, Copyright reserved, Reproduced by gracious permission of Her Majesty Queen Elizabeth II.

Let's look at a tree painted in 1908 by the Dutch artist, Piet Mondrian. What lines and colors do you see in *The Red Tree*?

Compare the lines in *The Red Tree* with the lines in *Study of a Tree* by Leonardo. Describe and compare the shapes of the two trees. Which picture looks like a real tree? Which picture is abstract?

Both pictures are thought to be masterpieces. But each is very different from the other. Each artist has a different **style**, or way of showing what is seen.

Piet Mondrian, The Red Tree, 1908, Oil on canvas, 31⅕″ × 38⅓″. Haags Gemeentemuseum, The Hague.

Creating Art

1. Go on a nature walk with your class to observe trees. Look closely at the lines created by the trunks and branches of the trees. Feel the texture of the bark. What colors do you see? What shapes do the trees have?

2. Make sketches of one or more of the trees you see. Think about the lines, colors, shapes, and textures.

3. Make a painting or crayon drawing of a tree. Include a variety of lines and colors. Think about the shape and texture of the tree. Your tree can be either realistic or abstract.

Art Materials	
Paper	Paint or crayons
Pencil	

Learning Outcomes

1. What does *style* mean to an artist?

2. Describe the lines, shapes, and textures in your picture of a tree.

3. Look at the trees on page 1. Compare the lines, shapes, and textures of these trees with the lines, shape, and textures of your tree.

93

43 Making Waves

Observing and Thinking

Tawaraya Sotatsu, Waves at Matsushima, *17th century, Paint on silk, 59⅞" × 141¼". Courtesy of the Freer Gallery of Art, Smithsonian Institution, Washington, D.C. 06.231*

Look at these two pictures of the ocean called **seascapes**. Both seascapes are by Japanese artists. One artist, Sotatsu, lived over three hundred years ago. The other artist, Hokusai, lived about one hundred fifty years ago.

Let's examine the older seascape first. It is a painting on silk. Is the ocean calm or active in the painting? What colors did the artist use for the ocean? What colors do you see in the land? What kinds of lines are in the painting? Trace some of the lines with your finger.

Look at the second seascape. It is a relief print. Describe the ocean in the relief print. What would it be like to be in one of the boats?

Find a part of the picture that is calm. The mountain, Mount Fuji, is a special place to the Japanese.

Hokusai, The Great Wave, *Japanese woodblock print, 14¾" wide. Trustees of the British Museum.*

Creating Art

1. Think about how the ocean looks. Make a picture in your mind. What kinds of lines do you see? What shapes do the waves make? What color is the water? What colors are the sky and land?

2. Use crayon on white construction paper to make a line drawing of the ocean. Make the waves have interesting lines and patterns. Do not use crayon to fill in the water. Do fill in the parts where you want land to be. Color in the sky.

3. Use a watercolor wash to fill in the water. First, use your paintbrush to spread water over your crayon drawing. Mix the paints to get the color you want. Use your paintbrush to spread the paint across the entire picture.

Art Materials

White construction paper	Paintbrush
	Watercolors
Small dish of water	Crayons

Learning Outcomes

1. What is a seascape?

2. What kinds of lines did you use in your seascape?

3. Compare the color of the ocean in your picture with the colors of the ocean in the two seascapes on these pages.

95

44 Putting Your Best Face Forward

Observing and Thinking

Examine this mask from Africa. What kinds of lines does it have? What shapes do you see? Which shapes are repeated? What kind of balance does the mask have?

African masks such as this one were made to be worn in ceremonial dances. It was believed that when a person put on the mask, he or she became powerful.

Bakuba Dance Mask, Congo. Collection of Mr. and Mrs. Robert Miner.

The masks had many different kinds of expressions. Some expressions were meant to frighten the people who watched the dance. Other expressions were meant to entertain the viewers.

What materials do you recognize in this mask? Which things are from nature? Which things were made by a person? Which parts were carved? Which parts were added?

Creating Art

1. You can make a papier-mâché mask; then decorate your mask with paint and things from nature, the way some Africans decorated their masks.

2. First, cut newspaper into ½ inch strips. Then blow up a balloon to be a little bigger than your head. Tie a knot in the end of the balloon to stop the air from escaping.

3. Next, dip a strip of newspaper into starch or very thin white glue. Then spread the wet strip out on the balloon. In this way, completely cover the balloon with strips of wet newspaper. Be sure to overlap the pieces of newspaper. Cover the balloon one more time so that it has at least two layers of newspaper on it.

4. Put your papier-mâché in a warm place to dry. Then collect things from nature to decorate your mask. You might want to use pebbles, beans and other kinds of seeds, leaves, or twigs.

5. When the newspaper is completely dry, use scissors to cut the back off the mask. Locate where your eyes will be on the mask. Poke holes in the mask so you can see when you put it on.

6. Use tempera paint to decorate the mask. Glue on the things from nature that you wish to use. Attach string or a rubber band to the mask to help keep it on your head.

Art Materials	THINK SAFETY
Newspaper	Things collected from nature
Scissors	
Balloon	White glue
Starch or very thin white glue	String or a rubber band
Tempera paint	

Learning Outcomes

1. What expressions did Africans sometimes use in their masks? Why?

2. What things from nature did you use to decorate your mask?

3. What kind of balance does your mask have?

45 The Nature of Their Art

Observing and Thinking

The art of the American Indians is as varied as the number of Indian nations. Yet all American Indian art has one thing that's the same. It is based on nature.

Most of the art is not realistic. The Indians changed the way nature made things look. Their art is abstract.

Look at the False Face mask of the Iroquois from the Northeast. Notice how the artist **distorted**, or twisted, the face.

Although the mask is of the face of a man, it has been changed. It is not like nature. It is abstract.

Study the Navajo sand painting from the Southwest. What kind of balance does it have? Describe the lines used in the sand painting.

What things from nature can you see in the painting? Are they realistic or abstract? Explain why.

Elon Webster, Iroquois False Face mask, 1937, Wood, metal, hair. Cranbrook Institute of Science, Bloomfield Hills, Michigan.

Sand paintings are made during Navajo ceremonies. Colored sand, made by crushing rocks, is sprinkled on the ground to make pictures and designs. The sand paintings are destroyed after the ceremony.

Creating Art

1. You can make a picture that looks similar to a Navajo sand painting. First, think of the things from nature that you would like to include. Think of ways you can change these things to make them abstract. Make some quick sketches of your ideas.

2. Decide on the kind of balance you want your picture to have. Then make a pencil sketch of your design on a piece of drawing paper.

3. Use crayon to draw your picture on a piece of sandpaper.

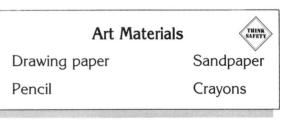

Art Materials THINK SAFETY

Drawing paper   Sandpaper

Pencil   Crayons

Learning Outcomes

1. What does *distorted* mean?

2. What colors and textures does your drawing have?

3. Look at the Chilkat blanket on page 16. It is a bear design. Is it realistic or abstract? Explain why.

99

46 Exploring Feelings in Pictures

Observing and Thinking

Vincent van Gogh, The Harvest. *National Museum Vincent van Gogh, Amsterdam.*

Study these landscape paintings by two artists who painted in the last half of the 1800s. Describe the colors in the two paintings.

Vincent van Gogh and Paul Gauguin used bright, pure colors in their paintings. Notice that both paintings have a feeling of calmness.

Study the lines in *The Harvest* by van Gogh. Notice the horizontal lines in the fields. Remember that horizontal lines show calmness. Find the vertical lines in

the fences. Remember that vertical lines show strength.

The Harvest is unusually calm for Vincent van Gogh's work. He painted it during a happy, untroubled part of his life. Most of his works are alive with movement.

Look at his painting, *The Starry Night,* on page 135. Let your finger trace the movement in the sky. The swirling lines show activity.

Like van Gogh, Paul Gauguin showed his feelings in his work. And like van Gogh, Gauguin had many troubles. He moved to Tahiti to get away from his problems. Tahiti was very calm. Gauguin's paintings show this calmness.

Paul Gauguin, Tahitian Landscape, 1891, Oil on canvas, 26¹¹/₁₆″ × 36⅜″. The Minneapolis Institute of Arts, the Julius C. Eliel Memorial Fund.

Creating Art

1. Think about a calm place. Imagine yourself sitting there feeling calm. Notice how quiet it is there.

   Now think of a loud, active place. Everything around you is moving.

2. Plan a painting of one of the places you imagined. If it is a calm place, make your picture show this calmness. If it is a loud, active place, make your picture show the movement.

   Think about the kinds of lines you will use in your picture. Do you want swirling lines to show activity? Or do you want horizontal and vertical lines to show calmness and strength?

   Use tempera paint to create a picture that shows calmness or activity.

Art Materials	
Tempera paint	Paper
Paintbrush	Paper towels
Small dish of water	Mixing tray

Learning Outcomes

1. Describe the lines you used in your painting.

2. Does your painting show calmness or activity? Explain why.

3. Study the painting on page 22. Does the picture show calmness or activity? Explain why.

47 *Once Again, with Feeling*

Observing and Thinking

Examine these two powerful paintings. Both were made in the early 1900s. Compare the shapes in the paintings. Which one has irregular shapes? Which has geometric shapes? Find and name at least seven geometric shapes in that painting.

Pablo Picasso, Three Musicians, 1921 (summer), Oil on canvas, 6'7" × 7'3¾". Collection, The Museum of Modern Art, New York. Mrs. Simon Guggenheim Fund.

Which painting shows things you can recognize? Find a guitar, sheets of music, and a clarinet. The name of this painting is *Three Musicians*. Find the shapes that suggest three people playing musical instruments. *Three Musicians* was painted by Pablo Picasso in 1921.

Find areas where bright colors were placed next to dark colors to create contrast. Look for parts that show rough textures. Which parts look smooth? Notice that rough and smooth areas were placed next to one another.

Vasily Kandinsky created this painting in 1912. Kandinsky believed that paintings should show what an artist feels inside. Many of the paintings he created were not meant to be pictures of real things. They were painted to show what Kandinsky felt inside.

What kinds of lines did Kandinsky use to show his feelings? What colors did he use?

Vasily Kandinsky, Improvisation 28 (Second Version), 1912, Oil on canvas, 43⅞" × 63⅞". Solomon R. Guggenheim Museum, New York.

Creating Art

1. Think about something that makes you angry or scared or very happy. Think about the colors and kinds of lines that might show your feelings. Are your lines thin and dancing or are they strong and bold? Are your colors light or dark? Are they warm or cool?

2. You can make a painting that expresses your inner feelings. First, use pieces of sponge dipped in paint. Choose colors that show how you feel. Press these sponges against your paper to leave prints of color.

3. When the sponge prints have dried, make lines across your paper. Use paint and a paintbrush to create these lines.

Art Materials	
Tempera paint	Paper
Small dish of water	Paintbrush
Pieces of sponge	

Learning Outcomes

1. Find the textures, lines, and shapes in your painting.

2. What colors did you use to express yourself in your painting?

3. Compare the way Kandinsky chose to express himself in his painting with the way Picasso expressed himself in *Three Musicians.*

Exploring Art

Costumes and Cultures

People from around the world have designed costumes for thousands of years. Their costumes tell us about the people who made them.

Peru.

Scotland.

Tunisia.

Examine the costumes on this page. What colors do you see? What textures were used in these colorful clothes? Which materials do you recognize? Why do you think people made their costumes out of the materials shown?

Some costumes were designed to meet the special needs of the environment. Which costume protects the face of its wearer from being sunburned?

What other things do these costumes tell you about the people who made and wear them?

Design a costume that tells others about the lifestyle you live. Think about the materials you might use. Think about what you want your costume to express about you. Draw your ideas on paper. You might want to gather the materials and make the costume you have designed.

Review

Using What You Have Learned

The artworks on this page are from different times and places. The ways of life of the people who made these artworks are very different. These differences helped to make the works of art what they are.

Flying Horse, *Eastern Han Dynasty, 2nd century A.D., 13½" × 17¾". Peoples Republic of China.*

Yellow Horse. Lascaux, France.

Vasily Kandinsky, Improvisation 28 (Second Version), *1912, 43⅞" × 63⅞". Collection, Solomon R. Guggenheim Museum, New York.*

1. Which is the oldest work of art? How can you tell? Which artwork was made most recently? How do you know this?

2. Which artwork is three-dimensional? What medium is it? What medium is each of the two-dimensional works? How can you tell?

3. Which two artworks are about the same subject? Name the subject. In what ways are these artworks alike? In what ways are they different? How does each one show movement?

4. Which artwork is not a picture of an object? What feelings does this work of art express to you?

Unit 4

Art Enriches Our Environment

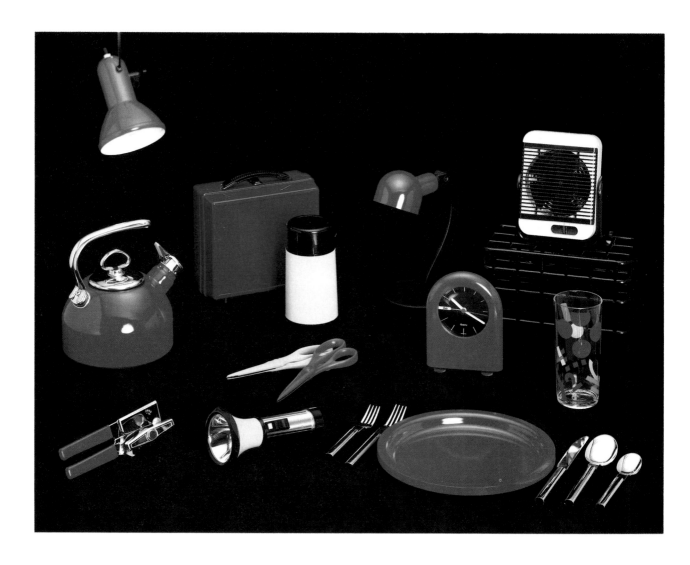

Which things in this picture do you use? What lines, shapes, colors, and textures can you find in these everyday works of art? Which things in this picture do you like? Tell why.

You are a **consumer**, or user, of art. Every day you make decisions about the art around you. You decide which clothes to wear, which pictures to hang in your room, how to arrange the dishes when you set the table.

In the United States and throughout the world, people are creating art right now. Many of these works of art are available for you to look at. Others are available for you to choose to live with.

Horace Pippin, Victorian Interior, *1946, Oil on canvas, 25¼″ × 30″. The Metropolitan Museum of Art, Arthur H. Hearn Fund, 1958.*

You can make better decisions about choosing the art around you if you understand art better. In this book you have studied the elements and principles of art. You have looked at and created works of art in many different media. You have learned about the art of the past.

In this unit, you will take a closer look at the art that is around you every day. You will study and create everyday works of art. You will experience the art that enriches the environment you live in.

48 Like No One Else Can

Observing and Thinking

Both of these sculptures are made from bronze. In what other ways are they alike? Two artists used the same materials to create sculptures of a seated man. In each the man is thinking. Yet the two works of art look quite different. Find some differences in the two sculptures.

Compare the textures of the two bronzes. Which sculpture looks heavier?

Wilhelm Lehmbruck, Seated Youth, 1918, Bronze, 41½" high. Collection, Wilhelm-Lehmbruck-Museum, Germany.

Auguste Rodin, The Thinker, 1880, Bronze, 27⅝" (height), 15" × 15" (base). The Metropolitan Museum of Art, Gift of Thomas F. Ryan, 1910. [11.173.9]

To create these forms, the artists shaped materials with tools. The way each artist uses his or her tools is called **technique**. No two artists have exactly the same technique. Each artist's technique is different. Only that person could have done it exactly that way.

Compare the techniques used to create the two sculptures on this page. Which artist worked by smoothing the surface of his sculpture? Which artist added lumps as he worked?

Creating Art

1. Use clay to make a sculpture of a person or an animal. You can model the sculpture or you can carve it.

2. Study the person or animal you have chosen. If you can, watch the person or animal. If the person or animal is not available to watch, look at pictures of your chosen subject.

3. Think about the techniques you will use to create your sculpture. Will you add clay in lumps, or will you smooth the clay? Will you cut away the clay in chunks, or will you carve delicate lines? Think about the texture you want

it to have. Plan the shape and balance of your work. Create your sculpture.

Art Materials	THINK SAFETY
Clay	Carving or modeling tools

Learning Outcomes

1. What does *technique* mean?

2. What techniques did you use to create your sculpture?

3. Compare the texture of your sculpture with the textures of the sculptures on these pages.

109

49 *On the Move*

Observing and Thinking

Did you know that the cars you ride in were designed by artists? These artists, called **industrial designers**, must know how a car works. They also must be able to make the cars have attractive shapes, lines, and balance.

Use your finger to trace the shapes and lines of this car. *Wildcat* was designed by William Porter and his assistants. They made *Wildcat* this shape so that it moves easily through the air.

Industrial designers also design other forms of transportation. The form of transportation on the right is the experimental aircraft, *Voyager*. The people who designed and made *Voyager* are trying to find new shapes and forms for machines that fly.

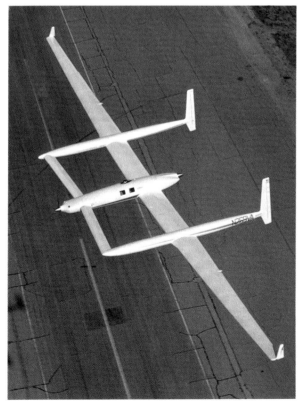

Creating Art

1. You can design a new form of transportation. Your idea can be for a machine that moves on land or on water or flies through the air.

2. Make several sketches of your idea. Think about its shapes and lines. Does it look attractive? Does it have balance?

3. Use charcoal or crayons to make your final drawing. Think of a name for your form of transportation.

Art Materials

Drawing paper

Pencil

Charcoal or crayons

Learning Outcomes

1. What is an industrial designer?

2. What new form of transportation did you design? In what ways is it different from other kinds of transportation?

3. What kinds of lines does it have? What kind of balance? Why did you make it the shape that it is?

50 *Picturing Books*

Observing and Thinking

Some artists create pictures that go in books. These pictures, or **illustrations**, help tell the stories in the books.

Maurice Sendak is an **illustrator** of children's books. He has created the pictures in many books for very young children.

Sendak created the picture below. It is from a book titled *Where the Wild Things Are*. What kinds of lines did the artist use?

Find at least three ways in which the artist showed texture. How did the artist show that it is nighttime?

Read the words below the picture. Notice that the picture helps make the words more understandable. Look at the picture to discover who was made king. Find a wild thing in the picture. Describe the wild thing.

and made him king of all wild things.

Maurice Sendak, And made him king of all wild things, from WHERE THE WILD THINGS ARE, Harper & Row, Publishers. Copyright © 1963 by Maurice Sendak.

and she saw many things that were strange and new.

Creating Art

1. Illustrate a story that you have written. The story can be for very young children. Or it can be for people your own age. Try to make your illustrations express your feelings about what you have written.

2. Choose the medium you will work in. Choose crayon, ink, felt pen, or paint. Decide how you want your characters to look. Think about what you want the settings, or places in the story, to look like. Consider how many words you want to go with each picture.

3. Think about the kinds of lines you will use. Think about the textures and colors. Plan each picture so that it has balance. Then create the illustrations for your story.

Art Materials	
Crayons, pens, felt pens, or paint	Paper

Learning Outcomes

1. What is an illustration?

2. How did you express your feelings in your illustrations?

3. Compare one of your illustrations with the illustration on this page. Compare the lines, the textures, and the colors.

113

51 *Wordy Pictures*

Observing and Thinking

Another way that artists work with pictures and words is by creating a picture with words. A **concrete poem** is a picture created by the shapes of words.

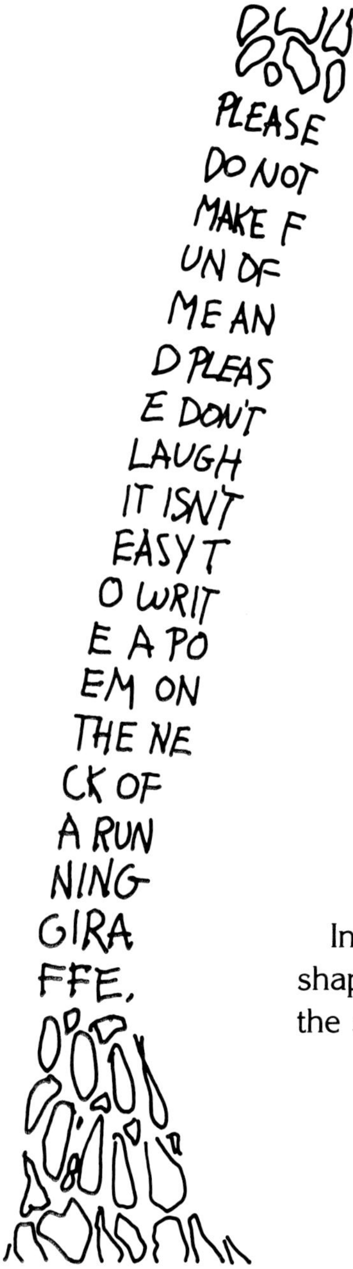

PLEASE
DO NOT
MAKE F
UN OF
ME AN
D PLEAS
E DON'T
LAUGH
IT ISN'T
EASY T
O WRIT
E A PO
EM ON
THE NE
CK OF
A RUN
NING
GIRA
FFE.

Study this concrete poem by Shel Silverstein. Describe the shape that the words have made. What does the artist want us to believe the shape is? Would the poem be funny if it was written in the shape of a regular poem? Would the illustration still be funny if it was simply a picture of a giraffe's neck without words?

In a concrete poem, the words and the shapes they make are both important to the success of the work.

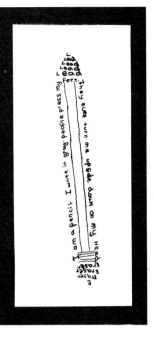

Creating Art

1. Study the concrete poems on this page. Then begin to plan your own concrete poem. You might want it to be about a kind of animal or about a place. Your words can be funny or they can tell how you feel about the animal or place. Write down a first draft, or copy, of your words.

2. As you choose the words for your concrete poem, think about the various shapes they can make. The words can make the outline of a shape or they can fill in the shape. You might want to make some quick sketches of your ideas.

3. Read the words you have chosen. Think about ways you can make the words better. When you know the exact words you want to use, choose the shape or shapes you want them to create. Use your best handwriting to create the letters and shapes in your concrete poem.

Art Materials	
Black felt pen	Paper

Learning Outcomes

1. What is a concrete poem?

2. What feelings does your concrete poem express?

3. Are the words and the shapes that they create both important in a concrete poem? Explain why.

52 A Comic Idea

Observing and Thinking

Artists communicate in many different ways. Some artists create **comic strips** or cartoons to show and tell about how they see things. You have probably read comic strips before. Have you ever wondered who created the pictures and words? Charles Schulz, a **cartoonist**, creates the words and pictures in *Peanuts.*

Examine the drawings in the comic strip. Describe Snoopy, the dog. Describe Woodstock, the bird, and Lucy, the girl. Charles Schulz made it easy for his readers to tell the characters apart.

Look closely to find the outlines of Snoopy, Woodstock, and Lucy. Notice that the outlines of the characters are filled with solid colors. The colors are intense, or very bright.

Study the words in the comic strip. How has the artist shown what the characters are saying? How can you tell which character is saying the words in the **balloons**, or white areas?

Notice that the backgrounds are plain. In a comic strip, the backgrounds have only what is needed to tell the story.

Charles Schulz, Peanuts, featuring "Good 'ol Charlie Brown." © 1978 United Feature Syndicate, Inc.

Kevin Dixey. Bhob Productions.

Creating Art

1. You can make a comic strip. First, think about a funny thing that has happened to you or someone you know. Think about different ways you can show and tell about the funny thing.

2. Decide which parts can be shown with pictures and which parts must be told with words. Try to use as few words as possible.

3. Think about the way you want your characters to look. You will probably want to keep the outlines of your characters simple. Remember that you will be making several drawings of the characters. Be sure to make each character look very different from the others. You want your readers to be able to tell the characters apart.

4. Make the sketches for your comic strip. Decide how the characters will look in each picture. What expressions will they have? Will they be standing or sitting still? Or will they be moving?

5. Study your sketches. Are the parts of the story shown in the best order? Are all the necessary parts of the story included? Then draw your final comic strip. Create the line drawings and add the words in the balloons. Make sure you use neat lettering so that your words are easy to read. Last of all, add the color.

Art Materials	
Paper	Crayons or felt pens
Pencil or black felt pen	

Learning Outcomes

1. What is a cartoonist?

2. Compare the expressions on the faces of the characters in your comic strip.

3. What makes your comic strip funny?

53 *Putting Your Stamp on It*

Observing and Thinking

Have you ever looked at a postage stamp and thought, "What an interesting picture"? Some people enjoy postage stamps so much they collect them.

Some stamps have pictures of things that most people have never seen. Other stamps have pictures of things we see every day.

Look at this stamp designed by a very young child. The **theme**, or subject, of the stamp is family unity. How did the child express family unity?

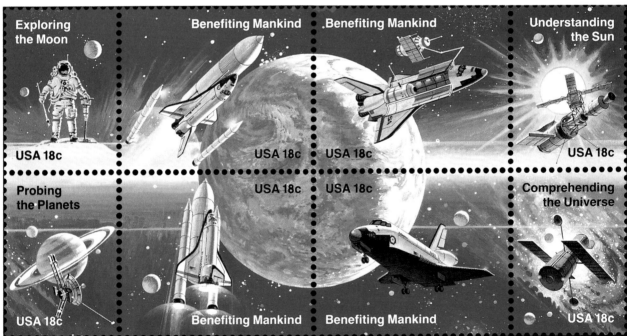

Most stamps have words as well as pictures. Read the words in the set of stamps above. What is the theme of the stamps?

Examine the pictures. What kinds of lines and shapes are used to create them?

What colors do you see? Find rough and smooth textures. Do all the parts of the set go together? Explain why the set of stamps has unity.

Creating Art

1. Design a postage stamp. First choose the theme of your stamp. What feelings do you want to express in your stamp? Then think about the medium you would like to use. You might choose crayons, felt pens, or paint.

2. Next, plan your picture and the words that will go with it. Think about the kinds of lines and colors you will use. Do you want your stamp to be horizontal or vertical? How will you balance the parts of the picture? Use pencil to make quick sketches of your ideas.

3. When your plans are finished, create your final piece of art. Be sure to include words with your picture.

Art Materials

Crayons, felt pens, or paint

Drawing paper

Pencil

Learing Outcomes

1. Compare the lines, colors, and textures in the stamps on this page.

2. Do the parts of your stamp have unity? Explain why.

3. What is the theme of your stamp? How did you express your feelings in the stamp you designed?

54 A Colorful Cloth

Observing and Thinking

African Batik, Kenya. *Private collection.*

Find light and dark areas on this piece of cloth. The dark against the light creates contrast.

The patterned cloth, or **batik**, was made with wax, dye, and a piece of cloth. To make a batik, wax is put on a piece of cloth. Some areas of cloth are not covered with wax. Then the waxed cloth is put into dye. The dye changes the color of the cloth in the areas where there is no wax. The dye cannot touch the cloth in the places where there is wax. Later the wax is removed.

The light areas of this batik were covered with wax. They show the color of the cloth before it was dyed.

The dark areas of the batik were not covered with wax. They show the colors of the dyes used. This batik was waxed and dyed more than one time.

What shapes do you see in this batik? What colors are the foreground shapes?

Batiks are used to make clothing, drapes, bedspreads, and other things we use every day. Some batiks are made to be framed and hung on walls.

120

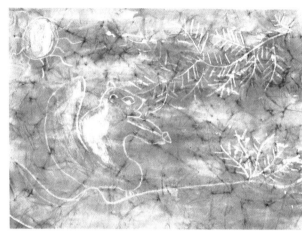

Creating Art

1. You can use crayon, paper, and water-colors to make a kind of batik. First, think about the picture or design you would like to create. Make sketches of your ideas.

2. Then use a white crayon to draw your picture or design on a piece of off-white construction paper. Fill in the areas that you want left light. Be sure to leave areas where there is no crayon.

3. Next, soak your paper in water. Then crumple it into a ball. Open up the paper and smooth it out. Wipe off the extra water with a paper towel.

4. Choose a dark shade of watercolor to paint your batik. Use a paintbrush to spread the paint across your paper. Describe what happens.

Art Materials	
Off-white construction paper	White crayon
	Watercolors
Small dish of water	Paintbrush
	Paper towel

Learning Outcomes

1. What is a batik?

2. In the kind of batik you made, what did you use in place of wax? What did you use in place of dye?

3. Does your batik have contrast? Explain why.

121

55 *Making Stencils*

Observing and Thinking

What is repeated on all the things you see below? These sailboats are prints made with a **stencil**, a design cut out of heavy paper. The cut piece of paper at the right is a stencil. First, the sailboat was drawn on the paper. Then the design was carefully cut out.

After a stencil is cut out, prints of it can be made. To make a print on a piece of paper, the stencil is placed on that paper. Next, a sponge is dipped into paint, then blotted on paper towel to get off the extra paint. The painted sponge is then pressed against the stencil. The paint goes through the holes cut into the stencil. Last of all, the stencil is carefully removed, and the print is left on the paper.

Creating Art

1. Think about a design you would like to make into a stencil. The design should be simple, like the outline of something. You can make several sketches on a piece of paper. Choose your favorite design. Then draw its outline on a piece of heavy paper.

2. Carefully cut out the outline. First, poke the scissors into the center of your outline. Then cut along the line that makes the outline.

3. Practice making prints. Lay your stencil on a piece of clean paper. Dip a sponge into thick tempera paint. Lightly blot the sponge on a paper towel to get off the extra paint. Then press the sponge against the stencil. Carefully lift the sponge. Try not to smear it across your paper. Repeat this several times. Then lift the stencil.

4. Use your stencil to make an interesting pattern. Stencil prints can be used to make cards or wrapping paper or to decorate a box.

Art Materials		THINK SAFETY
Paper	Scissors	
Pencil	Paper towels	
Heavy paper	Sponge	
Tempera paint		

Learning Outcomes

1. What is a stencil?

2. What outline shapes did you use to make your stencil?

3. How did you use your stencil to create a pattern?

56 *Fiddling Around*

Observing and Thinking

Did you know that the musical instruments in an orchestra or band are created by artists? Examine the two violins on this page. The one on the left was created by Antonio Stradivari, in 1701. Stradivari created some of the best violins ever made. Few of his fine instruments are left.

The colorful violin was created by a craftsman, Irving Sloane. This kind of violin is sometimes called a fiddle because of the way the musician chooses to play it. Compare Stradivari's violin to Irving Sloane's fiddle.

Antonio Stradivari, The Servais, cello. Smithsonian Institution, Washington, D.C.

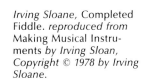

Irving Sloane, Completed Fiddle. reproduced from Making Musical Instruments *by Irving Sloan, Copyright © 1978 by Irving Sloane.*

The picture at the right shows an artist carving part of a violin. What part of the violin is he working on? What is this part of the violin made of?

Art Materials

Your choice of :

Two sticks and
  enamel paint,
  or

Oatmeal box,
  yarn, paint, and
  colored paper, or

Two paper
  plates, felt pens,
  six bottle caps,
  needle, and
  yarn

Creating Art

1. You can create a musical instrument. Choose one of the instruments shown above. Or design one of your own.

2. Collect the materials for the kind of instrument you wish to make. Put the materials together to create the instrument. Use paint, felt pens, and colored paper to decorate your instrument.

Learning Outcomes

1. What musical instrument did you make?

2. What kinds of lines, shapes, and colors did you decorate your instrument with?

3. In what ways are the two instruments on page 124 alike? In what ways are they different?

57 *Picturing Your Community*

Observing and Thinking

A group of people got together and decided to make a work of art that showed how they felt about their **community**, the neighborhoods where they live. Each person in the group created a picture that showed something about the New Canaan community. Each picture expressed the artist's feelings about the place.

Examine the pictures in this piece of art. What do some of the pictures show you? Which colors are repeated? What is the shape of every picture? What might the pictures be made of?

The pictures were made from pieces of fabric. The pieces of fabric were stitched together to make a kind of padded blanket, or **quilt**. Examine the texture of *The New Canaan Quilt*. Notice the lines that create patterns on the pieces of fabric. Tiny stitches make up the lines on the quilt. Tiny stitches also hold the pieces of fabric together.

Ann Price (designer), The "New Canaan Bicentennial" Quilt, made by the New Canaan Quilters. Illustration from QUILTING IN SQUARES by Katharine B. Fisher and Elizabeth B. Kay, Copyright © 1978 Katharine B. Fisher and Elizabeth B. Kay, Reprinted with the permission of Charles Scribner's Sons.

Creating Art

1. Your class can make a work of art that shows how you feel about your community. This work of art will be made of many pictures, like *The New Canaan Quilt*. Each person in your class can paint a picture that shows something about the neighborhoods you live in. You can put the pictures together to create a bulletin board.

2. First, each person must decide what part of your community to paint a picture of. Think about all the parts of your community. Share your ideas. Work together so that important parts of your community are not left out. Also, try not to have people repeat what others are doing.

3. Each person can plan and create his or her painting. Remember that all the paintings have to be made on pieces of paper that are the same shape and size. Make sure your painting expresses your feelings about the place you have chosen.

4. When all the paintings are dry, arrange them on a wall or bulletin board to make one large work of art.

Art Materials	
Paper	Tempera paint
Small dish of water	Paintbrushes

Learning Outcomes

1. What is a quilt?

2. What part of your community did you create a picture of? How did you express your feelings about this place?

3. Does your class work of art have unity? Explain why.

127

58 *Off the Wall*

Observing and Thinking

Diego Rivera, Fresco, 1931, 62¼" × 104¾". Photographed with permission of the Regents of University of California, Berkeley.

Diego Rivera created the above **mural,** or huge picture that covers an entire wall. The mural shows what it is like to be a member of a community of people who work in orchards.

Your classroom is a community of people who work as students. Your neighborhood is a community of people who live together. How is the community in Rivera's mural like the communities you live in? How is it different? What feelings did Rivera express in his mural?

Which people in the mural look closest? How did Rivera make these people look closer than the other people in the picture?

Creating Art

1. The community mural at the bottom of these pages was created by a classroom of students your age. What feelings did the students express about their community?

2. With your classmates, plan a mural that shows what it is like to live in your community. Be sure to include the places where people live, work, shop, play, and go to school.

3. Decide on the colors that the class will repeat throughout the mural to give it unity. What lines and shapes will be repeated?

   Plan a way for the people in your class to work. Can everyone work at once? Or should only part of the group work at one time?

4. Work together to make a chalk sketch of the picture on a huge piece of butcher paper. When the sketch is finished, you and your classmates can use felt pens or crayons to fill in the color and add details. Think about the kinds of lines and textures you want your part of the mural to have.

Art Materials	
Butcher paper	Felt pens or crayons
Yellow chalk	

Learning Outcomes

1. What is a mural?

2. Does your mural have unity? Explain why.

3. In what ways does your mural show how you feel about your community?

59 *Local Heroes*

Observing and Thinking

Sometimes artists create portraits of people they admire. Study these four portraits of Americans who have given to their communities. What media were used to create these portraits? Which portraits are two-dimensional? Which is three-dimensional?

Abraham Lincoln was President of the United States during the Civil War. He worked to keep our country together. Vinnie Ream Hoxie carved this sculpture of Lincoln out of marble. The statue stands in the Capitol in Washington, D.C.

Martin Luther King, Jr., was a man who worked to improve the ways in which people are treated. He wanted all people to be treated fairly. Robert Fitch took this photograph of King in his office.

A photographer also took this picture of Sally Ride. Sally Ride was the first American woman to go into space. She is an astronaut and a scientist.

Elaine de Kooning, Portrait of President John F. Kennedy, *1962–63, Oil on canvas, 64" × 46". The Harry S. Truman Library, Independence, Missouri.*

Elaine de Kooning painted this portrait of President John F. Kennedy. President Kennedy made plans to provide aid to poor areas of the country. He also started the U.S. Peace Corps.

Creating Art

1. Think of a person you admire for what he or she has given to your community. Perhaps the person has taken care of someone you know. Or perhaps the person risks his or her life to put out fires or to rescue people. Maybe you know someone who stands up for the rights of others.

2. Plan a portrait of the person you admire. Make several sketches of that person. Think about the expression you want the person to have. Decide on the medium you will use. You might choose clay, film and camera, paint, charcoal, or crayons.

3. Create a portrait of the person you admire for what he or she has given to

your community. Make your portrait show how you feel.

Art Materials	
Clay, film and camera, paint,	charcoal, or crayons

Learning Outcomes

1. What medium did you use? Is your portrait two-dimensional or three-dimensional?

2. Compare the expressions on the faces of your portrait and the portraits on these pages.

3. What feelings are expressed in your portrait?

131

60 Making a Friend

Observing and Thinking

Perhaps you know some of the puppets in this picture. Which puppets can you name?

Study the colors and textures of the puppets. What materials might some of the puppets be made of?

Puppets are designed by artists. Jim Henson, a **puppeteer**, designed the puppets above. Henson also works with the puppets to make them move and talk.

Creating Art

1. You can choose one of two kinds of puppets to make. You can use a paper bag to make a puppet. Or you can use a sock to make a puppet. A paper bag puppet is a kind of paper sculpture. A sock puppet is a kind of found-objects sculpture.

2. First, collect the material for the kind of hand puppet you wish to make. Then plan how you want the puppet to look. Think about the expression you want your puppet to have.

3. If you are making a paper-sculpture puppet, cut, bend, fold, curl, and tear the paper. Then glue the pieces to the paper bag.

    If you are making a found-objects puppet, you can glue or stitch the pieces to the sock.

4. Use felt pens to add details and texture to your puppet.

Art Materials ◆THINK SAFETY
Your choice of:

Paper sack, construction paper, and glue or	Sock, found objects, glue, needle, and thread

Learning Outcomes

1. What kind of puppet did you make?

2. What expressions can your puppet show?

3. What textures and shapes does your puppet have?

133

Exploring Art

Puppet Play

Puppet theaters exist throughout the world. Many communities have puppet theaters. Puppet theaters are in backyards, basements, and garages. A blanket over a table can be a puppet theater. A big box or several small boxes make excellent puppet theaters.

Perhaps you and some of your classmates would like to make a puppet theater. Collect the materials from your environment. Arrange the materials so they can be used as a theater. Then decorate the theater to make it attractive.

Write a puppet play to be performed in your theater. You can use the puppets you made in this unit or you can make some new ones.

Review

Using What You Have Learned

The Starry Night was created by Vincent van Gogh in 1889. It shows the intense emotion with which van Gogh made many of his works. The picture illustrates van Gogh's interest in the sky. Study *The Starry Night* as an art critic might.

Vincent van Gogh, The Starry Night, 1889, Oil on canvas, 29" × 36¼". Collection, The Museum of Modern Art, New York, Acquired through the Lillie P. Bliss Bequest.

1. What kinds of lines are in this work of art? Name two geometric shapes in the picture.

2. Point out the primary colors in the artwork. Name the two secondary colors in the picture. What intermediate colors do you see? Find tints and shades of blue.

3. What medium was used to create this work of art? How did the artist apply the medium?

4. How did van Gogh show texture in the trees? What other textures can you find?

5. Is the artwork realistic or abstract? Tell why. Is the picture calm or does it show movement? Explain why. What feelings are expressed in the artwork?

Glossary

abstract Not the way something really looks. An abstract work of art is based on a real object. But the artist leaves out details or changes the object in the picture to look different than the real object.

actual lines Lines you can see. (See *implied lines.*)

additive sculpture Sculpture made by adding materials to the work.

appliqué /a-plə-kā/ A picture or design created from pieces of fabric. The pieces of fabric are sewed or applied to a larger piece of fabric.

architect An artist who designs buildings.

architecture The art of designing and making buildings.

asymmetrical balance /ā-sə-me′-tri-kəl/ A kind of balance in which the two sides of a design are very different. A teapot is asymmetrical.

background The back part of a picture.

background shape The ground shapes in a picture. The background shapes are made by the edges of the foreground shapes.

balance An arrangement of parts so that they have equal force. Major types of balance are symmetrical, asymmetrical, and radial.

balloon The part of a cartoon or comic strip that holds the words. Balloons are most often white and are above the heads of the characters. Balloons also indicate who is saying or thinking the words.

batik /bə-tēk′/ A piece of cloth on which a pattern has been made with wax and dye. Wax is put on a piece of clean cloth. Then the waxed cloth is put into dye. The dye changes the color of the cloth in the areas where there is no wax. The wax is removed.

bronze A kind of metal from which sculptures are made. An artwork made of bronze.

caricature /kar′-i-kə-chur/ A picture in which features of the subject are exaggerated or changed. Animals made to act like people are caricatures.

cartoon A simple line drawing that tells a story. Cartoons often include words.

cartoonist An artist who creates the words and pictures in cartoons and comic strips.

carve To cut away pieces of a medium.

ceramic An artwork made from clay that has been fired in a kiln.

charcoal A soft medium used to make drawings. An artwork made with charcoal.

circle A two-dimensional, geometric shape.

cityscape A picture of a city.

clay A medium from which sculptures are made. Soft clay can be modeled, carved, coiled, or molded. Clay can be dried and hardened in the air or fired in a kiln.

collage /kə-läzh′/ A picture that is made of collected materials, such as bits of paper, pieces of fabric, and photographs.

color The hue of an object. Red, yellow, and blue are primary colors. Orange, green, and violet are secondary colors.

color wheel Shows relationships among colors. The color wheel shows the primary, secondary, and intermediate colors. The color wheel is sometimes divided into warm and cool colors.

comic strips Several cartoons, or simple pictures with words, that have been put together to tell a story.

community The area in which a person lives. A neighborhood is a kind of community. A nation is a larger community.

concrete poem A picture created by the shapes of words. The words and shapes in a concrete poem are both important. Without one or the other, the poem would not be as successful in giving its message.

cone A three-dimensional, geometric form.

consumer Someone who uses something.

contrast Differences or opposites placed next to or near each other in a picture. Putting dark next to light shows contrast.

cool color A color that gives the feeling of coolness. Yellow-green, green, blue-green, blue, blue-violet, violet, and red-violet are cool colors.

costume A special kind of clothing usually worn in ceremonies or at celebrations or festivals.

crayon A kind of medium used to make drawings. Crayons are usually made from wax.

crayon rubbing A design made by rubbing a crayon over a paper that has been placed on a textured surface. The crayon rubbing shows the textures.

credit The words below an artwork that is shown in a book or magazine. The credit gives information about the work of art, such as who created it, who owns it, and where it is located.

cross-stitch An embroidery stitch that looks like an X.

cube A three-dimensional, geometric form.

cylinder A three-dimensional, geometric form.

découpage A method of creating pictures by cutting and pasting pieces of painted paper.

detail A small or less important part.

diagonal A direction that a line can have. Diagonal lines suggest motion and activity.

distort To change the way something looks by twisting it or exaggerating some of its parts.

dome A half circle created with arches.

elements The building blocks of art. Line, shape and form, texture, space, value, and color are elements of art.

ellipse A two-dimensional, geometric shape.

embroidery A kind of stitchery made with yarn or thread on a piece of fabric.

emphasis /em'-fə-sis/ When an artist makes one part of a picture more important than another. Emphasis gets your attention.

expression The look on a person's face. A smile is an expression; so is a frown.

fabric A piece of cloth.

fired Baked at high temperatures in a special oven called a kiln.

foreground The front part of a picture.

foreground shapes The first shapes or figures in a picture.

form The three-dimensional shape of an object. Forms have many sides and viewpoints.

geometric Shapes, such as circles, squares, rectangles, triangles, ovals, and ellipses, and forms, such as cones, cubes, cylinders, rectangular forms, pyramids, and spheres. Most objects with geometric shapes and forms are made by people.

glaze The glassy coating put on clay. The glaze is fired to harden it. Glaze gives ceramics their color.

graphic A simple line drawing or illustration that gives a message.

horizon The line where the sky meets the ground.

137

horizontal A direction that a line can have. Horizontal lines are at rest. They are quiet and calm.

hue /hyoo/ The name of a color, such as blue, green, yellow, orange, red, and violet. Hue is another word for color.

illustration A picture that helps tell about something. The pictures in books are illustrations. They help make the words more clear.

illustrator A person who creates pictures that tell about something. The people who create the pictures in books and magazines are illustrators.

imagination Seeing something in a new way.

implied lines Lines you cannot see. Implied lines are hidden.

industrial designers Artists who create such works of art as cars and airplanes. These artists must know about the elements and principles of art. They must also know how different kinds of machines work.

ink A kind of medium used to make drawings. An artwork made with ink.

intensity The brightness or pureness of a color. A bright color is at its highest intensity. A dull color is at its lowest intensity.

intermediate color /in-tər-mē′-dē-ət/ A color made by mixing a secondary color with a primary color. Blue-green, yellow-green, yellow-orange, red-orange, red-violet, and blue-violet are the intermediate colors.

irregular shapes Shapes that are not geometric. Most shapes in nature are irregular. A leaf has an irregular shape.

kiln An oven that can reach very high temperatures. Kilns are used to fire clay.

landscape A view of outdoor scenery, such as mountains, rivers, fields, or forests.

lead A kind of soft metal. Lead is often used in stained glass. It holds together the pieces of colored glass.

line A path that a point has followed. Lines can be thick, thin, wavy, curling, straight, jagged, short, or long. Curving lines suggest restfulness. Jagged lines suggest movement.

line drawing A drawing made with lines and outlines, which can show textures, values, shapes, and forms.

marble A kind of stone from which sculptures can be carved. An artwork made of marble.

media The plural of medium. Ink, paint, and clay are kinds of media.

medium The kind of material from which an artwork is made.

model To form clay, or another soft material, with the hands.

mold A hollow form for shaping materials.

monoprint A kind of print made from a flat surface that has been painted. A piece of paper is pressed against the painted surface. The paint makes a picture on the paper. Only one print can be made of the picture painted on the flat surface.

mosaic /mō-zā′-ik/ A picture or design made of tiny pieces of material, such as colored tile, stone, or paper.

mural A huge picture that covers an entire wall. Usually murals are made directly on walls.

museum A place where works of art are displayed for people to look at. Museums take care of the artworks.

needlepoint A kind of stitchery made of very small stitches on a fabric screen.

neutral color A color that is not part of the color wheel. Black, gray, white, and brown are neutral colors.

opaque /ō-pāk′/ Not allowing light to go through. You cannot see through an object that is opaque.

outline   A line that shows the edge of an object. An outline is a closed line. Outlines show two-dimensional shapes.

oval   A two-dimensional, geometric shape.

overlap   When parts of a picture lie on top of other parts. Overlapping makes the parts on top look closer than the parts underneath.

palette   The tray or board on which colors are mixed.

papier-mâché /pā-per-mə-shā'/   Strips of paper dipped in paste or glue then molded into shapes. When the strips dry they are strong and solid.

pastel   A kind of crayon. Pastels can be made of oil or of charcoal. Oil pastels are like crayons; charcoal pastels are like chalk.

photographer   An artist who uses film and a camera to make pictures.

portrait   A picture of a person. Portraits tell about the people they are pictures of.

potter   An artist who works with clay. Potters can make dishes or sculptures.

primary colors   The colors from which all other colors are made. Red, yellow, and blue are the primary colors. The primary colors cannot be made by mixing other colors.

principles   Organize a work of art. The principles of art are the plans that make the elements come together. Balance, unity, emphasis, and rhythm are principles of art.

print   A mark left by an object that has been dipped in paint. Relief prints, monoprints, and stencils are kinds of prints.

puppet   A kind of doll that can be moved and made to look as if it were talking. Puppets are often made to act like people.

puppeteer   An artist who designs and works with puppets to make them move and talk.

pure colors   A color from the color wheel that has not been mixed with another color. Pure colors are intense.

pyramid   A three-dimensional, geometric form. Also the tomb of an Egyptian royal person or a building in South America on which ceremonies were held.

quilt   A kind of padded blanket made by stitching together pieces of fabric.

radial balance /rā'-dē-əl/   A kind of balance in which the design has a round center with parts that move away from it. A wheel has radial balance.

realistic   The exact way that an object really looks. A photograph usually looks realistic. Some paintings and drawings look realistic. (Compare *representational.*)

rectangle   A two-dimensional, geometric shape.

rectangular form   A three-dimensional, geometric form.

relief print   A kind of print made by carving away the parts that will not make a mark. The shapes that will be printed are left. Paint is applied to these shapes. Then the painted shapes are pressed against paper. The mark that is left is a relief print.

repetition   Repeating a part of or a pattern in a work of art. Repetition makes the parts of a picture come together.

representational   Very close to the way an object really looks. Many paintings and drawings are representational. They look similar to the way things really look.

rhythm /rith'-əm/   A repeated part or pattern in a picture.

running stitch   An embroidery stitch that is used to outline objects.

satin stitch   An embroidery stitch that is used to fill in objects.

sculpture A kind of three-dimensional art. Wood, paper, clay, bronze, wire, and marble are some of the materials used to make sculptures. Sculptures can be viewed from many sides.

seascapes Pictures of the ocean, seas, or large lakes.

secondary color A color made by mixing two primary colors. Green, orange, and violet are the secondary colors. Green is made by mixing blue and yellow. Orange is made by mixing red and yellow. Violet is made by mixing red and blue.

self-portrait A picture of oneself made by oneself. When you make a picture of yourself, you are making a self-portrait.

shade The color made by mixing a pure color with black. Shades are darker than pure colors. Shades have dark values.

shape The two-dimensional space between or around objects. Shapes are flat.

sphere A three-dimensional, geometric form.

square A two-dimensional, geometric shape.

stained glass Pieces of colored glass. Stained glass windows are made from these colored pieces of glass, which are held together with thin strips of lead.

stencil A design cut out of heavy paper. A stencil can be used to make a repeated print of the cutout design.

still life A picture of nonliving things. A picture of a bowl of fruit is a still life.

stitchery A kind of artwork made with a needle and thread.

studio The workplace of an artist. A studio might be a room in a building or an entire building. The artist keeps equipment and materials in the studio.

style The way of showing or expressing what is seen.

subtractive sculpture Sculpture made by cutting or carving away some of the material from which the artwork is made.

symbol Something that stands for or represents another thing. A horse is a symbol of power and majesty.

symmetrical balance /sə-me′-tri-kəl/ A kind of balance in which both sides of a design are exactly alike. The wings of a butterfly are symmetrical.

tapestry A heavy woven cloth made to hang on a wall.

technique /tek-nēk′/ The way an artist uses his or her tools. No two artists have exactly the same technique.

tempera /tem′-pə-rə/ A kind of medium used to make paintings. Tempera is an opaque paint; you cannot see through it. An artwork made with tempera.

textile Artworks made from cloth or yarn. Weavings, tapestries, stitcheries, appliqués, and quilts are kinds of textiles.

texture The way an object feels when you touch it. Texture can be seen as well as felt. Rough and smooth are kinds of textures.

theme The subject of a work of art.

three-dimensional Having many sides. A shoe is three-dimensional; it has a top, a bottom, a front, a back, a left side, and a right side. Three-dimensional objects have height, length, and width.

tint The color made by mixing a pure color with white. Tints are lighter than pure colors. Tints have light values.

transparent Having the ability to let light through. You can see through an object that is transparent.

triangle A two-dimensional, geometric shape.

two-dimensional Flat. A painting is two dimensional. It has two sides: a front and a back. But only one side has a picture. Two-dimensional objects have height and length.

unity When the parts of a picture come together. Each part fits with the others.

value Refers to the lightness and darkness of what is seen. The amount of light reflected from a surface gives it its value. White is the lightest value; black is the darkest. Colors have value. Tints are lighter values of pure colors. Shades are darker values of pure colors.

vertical A direction that a line can have. Vertical lines are strong. They are firm and give support.

viewpoints Sides from which an object can be seen. A shoe has many viewpoints; if you put a shoe on a table you can move around the table to see different views of the shoe.

warm color A color that gives the feeling of warmth. Yellow-green, yellow, yellow-orange, orange, red-orange, red, and red-violet are warm colors.

wash A very thin coat of paint. Washes are often made with water and a small amount of watercolor.

watercolor A kind of medium used to make paintings. Watercolor is a transparent paint; you can see through it. An artwork made with watercolors.

weaving A kind of textile made by putting threads over and under one another.

Artists' Reference

All the works by famous artists presented in this book are listed here. Use this list to locate particular paintings, drawings, sculptures, and other artworks and to find works by artists who especially interest you.

Ashevak, Kenoujauk   *The Return of the Sun* 64

Bonnard, Pierre   *The Breakfast Room* 20

Calder, Alexander   *The Hostess* 81

Cézanne, Paul   *Flowers in a Glass Vase* 73

Chagall, Marc   *I and the Village* 10, 35

da Vinci, Leonardo   *Study of a Tree* 92

Degas, Edgar   *Portrait of Edmond Duranty* 52

de Kooning, Elaine   *Portrait of President John F. Kennedy* 131

de Predis, G. A.   *Portrait of Beatrice d'Este* 18

Dürer, Albrecht   *Study of a Dog* 12

Fitch, Robert   *Portrait of Martin Luther King, Jr.* 130

Gauguin, Paul   *Tahitian Landscape* 101

Greig, Evangeline   untitled needlepoint 60

Hokusai   *The Great Wave* 95

Hoxie, Vinnie Ream   *Lincoln* 130

Kandinsky, Vasily   *Improvisation 28* 103, 105

Lehmbruck, Wilhelm   *Seated Youth* 108

Liotard, Jean-Etienne   *Still Life* 58

Lundeberg, Helen   *Desert Coast* 23

Matisse, Henri   *The Purple Robe (and Anemones)* 2
                         The Sorrow of the King 72

Mondrian, Piet   *Composition with Red, Blue, and Yellow* 24
                         The Red Tree 93

Monet, Claude   *Palazzo da Mula, Venice* 22

O'Keeffe, Georgia — *Barn with Snow* (facing page 1)
Canyon with Crows   42

Picasso, Pablo — *Bull's Head*   32
The Jester   50
Three Musicians   102
The Violin and Compote of Fruit   62

Pippin, Horace — *Victorian Interior*   107

Rivera, Diego — untitled mural   128

Rodin, Auguste — *The Thinker*   108

Schulz, Charles — *Peanuts featuring "Good ol' Charlie Brown"*   116

Sendak, Maurice — from *Where the Wild Things Are*   112

Sesshū (Tōyō) — *Winter Landscape*   40

Sheeler, Charles — *Pertaining to Yachts and Yachting*   30

Silverstein, Shel — from *Where the Sidewalk Ends*   114

Sloane, Irving — *Completed Fiddle*   124

Sotatsu, Tawaraya — *The Waves at Matsushima*   94

Stradivari, Antonio — *The Servais*   124

Toba Sōjō (Toba, Abbott) — *Animal Caricatures*   6

Toulouse-Lautrec, Henri de — *A Corner of the Moulin de la Galette*   26

van Gogh, Vincent — *The Harvest*   100
The Starry Night   135

von Herkomer, Sir Hubert — *Head of an Old Man*   54

Webster, Elon — Iroquois False Face mask   98

Wyeth, Andrew — *That Gentleman*   56

Index

A

Abstract art, 63, 93, 98, 99, 102, 135
Adair, Jim
  Boy in Orange Slicker on Green Bench, 28
Aircraft, 110, 111
Altamira cave paintings, 76
Animals in art, 6, 12, 32, 33, 76, 84, 85, 105, 109, 114, 115; artworks of, 3, 6, 7, 12, 16, 33, 76, 84, 85, 105, 109, 114, 115
Apollo Belvedere, 80
Appliqué, 70, 71
Architecture, 68, 69, 74, 78, 86, 90
Art; African, 73, 96, 97, 104, 120; American, viii, 23, 30, 42, 44, 56, 60, 81, 83, 107, 110, 112, 114, 116, 118, 124, 126, 130, 131, 132; American Indian, 16, 98, 99; Chinese, 84, 85; comparing old and new, 74, 75, 77, 81, 83, 87, 89, 91, 93, 95; credits, 73; definition of, 1; Dutch, 24, 93, 100, 101, 135; Eastern European, 86, 87; Egyptian, 78, 79; English, 70; elements of, 1, 107 (*see also* names of elements); Eskimo, 48, 64; French, 2, 20, 22, 26, 27, 52, 58, 72, 73, 90, 100, 101, 108; German, 12, 68, 103, 105, 108; Greek, 80, 81; Inca Indian, 88, 89; Italian, 18, 44, 92, 93; Japanese, 6, 40, 94, 95; materials, 34, 36, 37, 40, 50, 58, 104, 108, 132 (*see also* each kind of material); Mexican, 68, 128; prehistoric, 6, 76, 105; principles of, 1, 107; (*see also* names of principles); Renaissance, 92; Roman, 82, 83; Russian, 10, 35, 103, 105; South American, 88, 89, 104; Spanish, 32, 39, 50, 62, 63, 76, 102, 103
Artists, 1, 37 (*see also* names of artists); architects, 69; cartoonists, 116; engineers, 88; illustrators, 112; industrial designers, 110, 111; instrument makers, 124; as observers, 56, 92; painters, 36, 37; photographers, 28, 37, 46, 130; potters, 84; puppeteers, 132; quilters, 126; sculptors, 37; techniques of, 43, 108; textile designers, 89; weavers, 66, 88; workplaces of, 37

Ashevak, Kenoujauk
  The Return of the Sun, 64
Asymmetrical balance, 16, 17, 25, 58

B

Background, 17, 27, 64, 65, 87, 116, 120
Background shapes, 14, 15, 64, 65
Bakuba Dance mask, 96
Balance, 1, 35, 59, 66, 67, 82, 87, 91, 96, 98, 99, 109-111, 113, 119; asymmetrical, 16, 17, 25, 58; defined, 16; radial, 17, 90; symmetrical, 16, 17, 58, 79
Batik, 120, 121
Bonnard, Pierre
  The Breakfast Room, 20
Book illustrations, 72, 73, 113, 114
Bridges, 82, 83
Bronze sculpture, 50, 73, 80, 84, 108
Buildings; Cathedral of Notre Dame, 90; constructing models of, 69; designing, 69, 71, 72; John Hancock Tower, 74; Neuschwanstein Castle, 68; Santa Sophia, 86; Trinity Church, 74

C

Calder, Alexander
  The Hostess, 81
Cameras, 46, 47, 131
Careers (*see* Artists)
Caricatures, 6, 7
Castles, 68
Cathedral of Notre Dame, 90
Cave paintings, 6, 76, 105
Ceramics, 72, 84
Cézanne, Paul
  Flowers in a Glass Vase, 73
Chagall, Marc
  I and the Village, 10, 35
Charcoal, 52, 53, 111
Charioteer of Delphi, 80
Chilkat blanket, 16, 99
Cityscapes, 17

Clay, 50, 51, 84, 89, 109, 131

Clothing, 104, 106

Collage, 62; creating a, 31, 63, 70, 71

Color, viii, 1, 39, 62, 63, 66, 67, 71, 77, 83, 86-88, 91, 93-95, 104, 106, 113, 117-120, 125, 126, 129, 132; brightness of, 24, 25, 35, 90, 100-103, 116; cool, 22, 23, 89, 103; defined, 20; dullness of, 24, 25, 102; emphasis and, 28; hues, 20, 27; intensity of, 24, 25, 116; intermediate, 20, 21, 27, 35, 135; mixing, 20, 21, 26, 27, 57; neutral, 23; primary, 20, 27, 35, 135; pure, 24, 27, 100, 101; secondary, 20, 27, 35, 135; shades, 26, 27, 35, 70, 121, 135; tints, 26, 27, 35, 70, 135; value, 26, 27, 35, 70, 102, 103, 120, 135; warm, 22, 23, 89, 103

Color value, 26, 27, 35, 70, 102, 103, 120, 135

Color wheel, 20-22

Comic strips, 116, 117

Community art, 126-131

Computer graphics, 77

Concrete poem, 114, 115

Consumer of art, 107

Contrast, 18, 120

Cool colors, 22, 23, 89, 103

Coronado Bay Bridge, 82, 83

Costumes, 104

Crayons, 13, 19, 23, 29, 39, 44, 45, 77, 95, 99, 111, 113, 119, 121, 129; rubbings with, 13

Credits, defined, 73

D

Da Vinci, Leonardo, 18, 44, 92, 93
  Study of a Tree, 93

Découpage, 72

Degas, Edgar
  Portrait of Edmond Duranty, 52

De Kooning, Elaine
  Portrait of President John F. Kennedy, 131

De Predis, G.A.
  Portrait of Beatrice d'Este, 18

Design, 62, 65-67, 87, 88, 91; geometric, 88, 89; graphic, 76, 77; industrial, 110

Designing; bridges, 82, 83; buildings, 69, 71, 72; on cloth, 88, 89; costumes, 104; forms of transportation, 110, 111; graphics, 77; musical instruments, 124, 125; postage stamps, 118, 119; puppet theaters, 134; puppets, 132, 133; stained glass, 90, 91; stencils, 122, 123

Details in artworks, 12, 17, 23, 27, 31, 39, 45, 51, 54, 57, 61, 73, 85, 92, 129, 133

Diagonal lines, 4, 5, 35

Dimensions, 38, 39, 48-50, 69, 73, 79, 105, 130, 131

Distance, showing, 30, 31, 44, 45, 58, 59, 70, 71, 73, 128

Distortion, 98, 99

Drawing; with chalk, 57, 59, 129; with charcoal, 52, 53, 111, 131; with crayon, 19, 23, 29, 39, 44, 45, 53, 59, 77, 89, 95, 99, 111, 113, 119, 129, 131; comic strips, 116, 117; with felt pen, 17, 77, 79, 89, 113, 115, 117, 119, 129; with ink, 40, 41, 113; landscapes, 23, 40, 41, 44, 45; from nature, 3, 41, 93; with pastels, 58, 59; with pencil, 5, 7, 19, 39, 41, 45, 53, 61, 77, 79, 81, 83, 87, 92, 99, 104, 115, 117, 119, 121, 123, 131; portraits, 53, 57, 131; seascapes, 95; sketches, 5, 7, 19, 39, 41, 45, 53, 57, 61, 77, 79, 81, 83, 87, 92, 99, 104, 115, 117, 119, 121, 123, 129, 131; still lifes, 59; textures, 13, 41, 52, 53, 58, 59, 92, 93, 99; three-dimensional objects, 39; trees, 45, 93

Drawings, 40, 41, 44, 45, 52, 53, 58, 59, 72, 76, 77, 92, 113, 116, 117

Dürer, Albrecht
  Study of a Dog, 12

E

Elements of art, 1, 107 (*see also* names of elements)

Embroidery, 60, 61

Emphasis, 28, 29, 35

Expression in art, 46-49, 56, 57, 96, 100-105, 117, 131, 133 (*see also* self expression)

F

Fabric design, 66, 67, 88, 120, 121, 126

False Face mask, 98

Felt pen, 17, 77, 79, 113, 115, 119, 125, 129

Film and cameras, 46, 47, 131

Firing, 84

Fontana, Franco
  Reflected Reeds, 3

145

Foreground, 17, 64
Foreground shapes, 14, 15, 64, 65, 120
Form, 69, 85, 86, 108
Found objects, 15, 32, 33, 133

G

Gauguin, Paul
　Tahitian Landscape, 101
Geometric shapes, 8-11, 24, 25, 31, 35, 58,
　88, 89, 102, 135
Glass, stained, 90, 91
Glaze, 84
Gold, 79, 88
Graphics, 76, 77
Greek art, 80
Greig, Evangeline
　untitled work, 60

H

Henson, Jim, 132
History: African, 96, 97, 104; American, 60,
　68, 74, 75, 77, 81, 83; American Indian, 98,
　99; cave paintings, 6, 76, 105; Chinese, 84,
　85; comparing old and new art, 74, 75, 77,
　81, 83, 87, 89, 91, 93, 95; Congo, 96, 97;
　Cubism, 102; Dutch, 93, 100, 101, 135;
　Eastern European, 86, 87; Egyptian, 78,
　79; Eskimo, 48; Expressionism, 103;
　French, 66, 72, 90; German, 68, 103, 105;
　Greek, 80, 81; Inca Indian, 88, 89; Italian,
　92, 93; Japanese, 94, 95; Mexican, 68; Mid-
　dle Ages, 66, 68; Peruvian, 88, 89, 104;
　Post-Impressionism, 100, 101; Renais-
　sance, 92; Roman, 82, 83; Russian, 10, 35,
　103; Scottish, 104; South American, 88,
　89, 104; Spanish, 76, 102, 103; Tunisian,
　104
Horizon, 45
Horizontal lines, 4, 5, 45, 100, 101, 119
Hoxie, Vinnie Ream
　Lincoln, 130
Hudson River, Quilt, The, 126
Hues, 20, 27

I

Ife Head of a King, 73
Illustrations, 112, 113
Imagination and art, 1, 32, 33
Implied lines, 10, 11, 35

Inca Indians, 88, 89
Inca Poncho with Geometric Design, 88
Ink drawings, 40, 41, 113
Intermediate colors, 20, 21, 27, 35, 135
Iroquois False Face mask, 98
Irregular shapes, 8, 9, 40, 58, 70, 102

J

John Hancock Tower, 74

K

Kandinsky, Vasily
　Improvisation 28, 103, 105
Kennedy, John F., 131
Kenyan batik, 120
Kiln, 84
King, Martin Luther, Jr., 130

L

Landscapes, 23, 40-45, 73, 100, 101
Lascaux cave paintings, 6, 76, 105
Lead, 90, 91
Lehmbruck, Wilhelm
　Seated Youth, 108
Light and art, 18, 19
Lincoln, 130
Lines, viii, 1, 12, 17, 24, 27, 30, 39, 40, 41, 52,
　54, 55, 62, 77, 79, 82, 93, 96, 98, 106, 110-
　113, 117, 118, 123, 125; actual, 10; at rest,
　2, 4, 5; creating moods with, 2-5, 100, 101,
　103; creating motion with, 2-5, 84, 85, 94,
　95, 100, 101, 105; defined, 2, 10; diagonal,
　4, 5, 35; directions of, 4, 5; emphasis and,
　28; horizontal lines, 4, 5, 45, 100, 101, 119;
　implied, 10, 11, 35; kinds of 2, 6, 92, 135;
　vertical, 4, 5, 100, 101, 119
Living with art, 106, 107, 110, 112, 118-120,
　122-126, 129-134
Liotard, Jean-Etienne
　Still Life, 58
Lundeberg, Helen
　Desert Coast, 23

M

Marble, 80, 130
Masks; African, 96; American Indian, 98;
　Bakuba Dance, 96; creating, 49, 79, 97;
　Eskimo, 48; Egyptian, 78, 79; False Face
　mask, 98; Tutankhamen's Burial, 78, 79

146

Materials, art, 34, 36, 37, 40, 50, 58, 104, 108, 132

Matisse, Henri
  découpage, 72
  The Purple Robe, 2
  The Sorrow of the King, 72

Media, 40, 42, 43, 130

Medium, 40, 41, 73, 105, 119, 131, 135

Michelangelo, 44

Mission, Rancho de Taos, 68

Modeling, clay, 50, 51, 85

Mondrian, Piet
  Composition with Red, Blue, and Yellow, 24
  The Red Tree, 93

Monet, Claude
  Palazzo da Mula, Venice, 22

Monoprints, 54, 55

Mosaics, 86, 87

Motion, in art, 2-5, 84, 85, 94, 95, 100, 101, 105, 135

Mount Fuji, 94

Muench, Davio
  Forest Floor, 8
  Ocotillo and Prickly Pear Cactus, 3

Murals, 128, 129

Museums, art, 73, 75

Musical instruments, 124, 125

N

Nature, 1, 3, 6-9, 12, 93, 96-99

Navajo sand painting, 98, 99

Needlepoint, 60

Neuschwanstein Castle, 68

New Canaan Quilt, 126

Nonobjective art, 21, 103, 105

Notre Dame, Cathedral of, 90

O

Obreski, George
  Bicycle and Wall, 16

O'Keeffe, Georgia
  Barn with Snow, viii
  Canyon with Crows, 42

Opaque paints, 56, 57

Outlines, 6, 7, 10, 17, 40, 41, 43, 60, 61, 65, 76, 77, 115, 123

Overlapping, 11, 21, 63, 73, 97; to show distance, 30, 31, 44, 45, 58, 59, 70, 71, 128

P

Painting; applying dark and light colors, 42, 43, 56, 57; feelings, 100, 101, 103; landscapes, 42, 43, 83, 100, 101; mixing colors in, 20, 21, 26, 27, 43; portraits, 46, 47, 52, 55, 57, 130, 131; sand, 98, 99; with sponges, 103; with tempura, 27, 56, 57, 83, 97, 101, 113, 119, 125, 127, textures, 27, 43, 57, 83, 102, 135; with watercolors, 17, 21, 42, 43, 56, 95, 113; watercolor washes, 17, 43, 95, 119;

Paintings, viii, 2, 6, 10, 18, 20, 22-24, 26, 30, 35, 36, 42, 56, 57, 72, 73, 76, 93, 94, 100-103, 105, 128, 131

Palette, 26

Paper arrangements, 11, 17, 25, 31, 62, 63, 72, 87, 91

Paper construction, 49, 133

Papier-mâché, 97

Pastels, 58, 59

Patterns in art, 88, 89, 95, 123, 126

Photographs, 1, 3-5, 8, 12, 16, 17, 19, 28, 46, 47, 127, 130, 131

Photography, 28, 39, 46, 47, 73, 130, 131

Picasso, Pablo
  Bull's Head, 32, 39
  The Jester, 50
  Three Musicians, 102, 103
  The Violin and Compote of Fruit, 62, 63

Pippin, Horace
  Victorian Interior, 107

Poetry, concrete, 114, 115

Pont du Gard, 82

Porter, William
  Wildcat, 110

Portraits, 46, 47, 50-57, 73, 109, 130, 131

Prehistoric art, 6, 76

Primary colors, 20, 27, 35, 135

Principles of art, 1, 107 (*see also* names of principles)

Prints; found-objects, 14, 15; monoprints, 54, 55; potato, 65; relief 64, 65, 94, 95; stencil, 122, 123;

Postage stamps, 118

Puppeteers, 132

Puppets, 132-134

Puppet theater, 134

Pure colors, 24, 27, 100, 101

Pyramids, 78, 79

Q

Quilts, 126, 127

R

Radial balance, 17, 90
Realistic art, 93, 98, 135
Relief prints, 64, 65, 94, 95
Repetition in design, 30, 31, 88, 89, 96, 122, 126, 129
Representational, 84, 93
Rhythm, 1, 30, 31, 88, 89
Richmond, England, 70
Rivera, Diego
    untitled mural, 128
Rodin, Auguste
    The Thinker, 108
Rose window, 90
Rubbings, crayon, 13

S

Sally Ride, 131
Sand painting, 98, 99
Santa Sophia, 86
Schulz, Charles
    Peanuts, featuring Good 'ol Charlie Brown, 116
Sculpting, 32, 33, 48-51, 81, 84, 85, 97, 108, 109, 131
Sculpture; animal, 32, 33, 84, 85; bronze, 50, 80, 84, 108; clay, 51, 57, 84, 85, 109, 131; found-objects, 32, 33, 96, 97, 133; Greek, 80, 81; marble, 80, 130; movement in, 84, 85; paper, 49, 133; papier-mâché, 97; subtractive, 48, 49, 85, 96, 109; texture in, 50, 51, 80, 84, 85, 108; three-dimensional, 39, 48, 49; wire, 81
Seascapes, 94, 95
Secondary colors, 20, 27, 35, 135
Self-portrait, 55
Self expression 100-105, 108, 109, 113, 115, 116, 118, 119, 126-128, 129, 135
Sendak, Maurice
    from *Where the Wild Things Are,* 112
Sesshū
    Winter Landscape, 40
Shades, 26, 27, 35, 70, 135
Shadow, 18, 19, 27
Shape, viii, 1, 17, 30, 39, 41, 53-55, 57, 60, 63, 70, 71, 77, 82, 87, 90, 91, 93, 95, 96, 106, 108, 110, 111, 114, 115, 118, 119, 125-127, 129, 133; background, 14, 15, 64, 65; defined, 8; foreground, 14, 15, 64, 65, 120; geometric, 8-11, 24, 25, 31, 35, 58, 88, 89, 102, 103, 135; irregular, 8, 9, 40, 58, 70, 102; in nature, 8, 9
Sheeler, Charles
    Pertaining to Yachts and Yachting, 30
Silverstein, Shel
    from *Where the Sidewalk Ends,* 114
Size, 63; to show emphasis, 29; to show distance, 44, 45, 70, 71, 128
Sketches, 5, 7, 19, 39, 41, 45, 53, 57, 61, 77, 79, 81, 83, 87, 92, 99, 104, 115, 117, 119, 121, 123, 129, 131
Sloane, Irving
    Completed Fiddle, 124
Sotatsu, Tawaraya
    Waves at Matsushima, 94
Space; dimensions, 38, 39, 48-50, 69, 73, 79, 105, 130, 131; distance, 30, 31, 44, 45, 70, 71, 73, 128
Sponge painting, 103
Stained glass, 72, 90, 91
Stamps, postage, 118, 119
Stencils, 122, 123
Still lifes, 27, 29, 58-61, 73
Stitchery, 60, 61, 126, 127, 133
Stradivari, Antonio
    The Servais, 124
Student art, 7, 9, 11, 14, 25, 29, 31, 33, 39, 41, 43, 45, 47, 49, 51, 53, 57, 59, 61, 63, 65, 67, 71, 79, 87, 91, 97, 109, 111, 113, 115, 119, 121, 123, 128-129, 133
Studio, 37
Style in art, 93
Sund, Harald
    Street Scene, 1
    Tulip Fields, 4
Symbols, 79, 84, 85
Symmetrical balance, 16, 17, 58, 79

T

Tapestries, 66, 67, 72
Techniques, 43, 108, 109
Tempera, 15, 27, 55-57, 65, 83, 97, 101, 113, 119, 123, 125, 127
Textiles, 16, 60, 61, 66, 67, 70, 71, 88, 89, 120, 121, 126, 127
Texture, 1, 39, 70, 71 104, 106, 109, 112, 113, 118, 119, 126, 129, 132, 133; char-

coal and, 52; in collages, 62, 63; crayons and, 13; definition of, 12; drawing, 13, 41, 52, 53, 58, 59, 92, 93, 99; in paintings, 27, 43, 57, 83, 102, 135; in prints, 58; in sculpture, 50, 51, 80, 84, 85, 108; in weaving, 67

Themes in art, 118

Three-dimensional art, 38, 39, 48-50, 69, 73, 79, 105, 130, 131

Three-dimensional forms, 69, 86

Tints, 26, 27, 35, 70, 135

Tissue paper, 31, 91

Tlingit Indians
  Chilkat Blanket, 16, 99

Toba Sōjō
  Animal Caricatures, 6

Tools, art, 34, 108

Toulouse-Lautrec, Henri
  A Corner of the Moulin de la Galette, 26

Transparent paints, 42, 43

Transportation, 110, 111

Trees, 93

Trinity Church, 74

Two-dimensional art, 39, 50

Tutankhamen, 78

U

The Unicorn in Captivity, 66

Unity in art, 1, 30, 62, 118, 119, 127, 129

V

Value, viii, 1, 18, 19, 120, 135, color, 26, 27, 35, 42, 120, 135

Van Gogh, Vincent
  The Harvest, 100
  The Starry Night, 100, 135

Vertical lines, 4, 5, 100, 101, 119

Viewpoints in art, 38, 39, 48, 85, 107

Von Herkomer, Sir Hubert
  Head of an Old Man, 54

Voyager, 110

W

Warm colors, 22

Washes, painting, 17, 43, 95

Watercolors, 17, 21, 42, 43, 56, 95, 113, 120

Weaving, 66, 67, 88

Webster, Elon
  Iroquois False Face mask, 98

Where the Sidewalk Ends, 114

Where the Wild Things Are, 112

Windows, stained glass, 90

Wire sculpture, 81

Words in art, 112-119

Wyeth, Andrew, 56
  That Gentleman, 56

Y

Yarn, 61, 67

Acknowledgments

We gratefully acknowledge the valuable contributions of the following artists, consultants, editorial advisors, and reviewers who participated in the development of this book: Ruth Jones and C.K. Greenwald, teachers, St. Luke's Lutheran Day School, La Mesa, California; Mirta Golino, art educator and editorial advisor, San Diego; Jeff Jurich, animator and writer, Celluloid Studios, Denver; Dennis Smith, sculptor, Highland, Utah; Virginia Gadzala, costume designer, San Diego; Phyllis Thurston, former Art Supervisor, Pinellas County School District, Clearwater, Florida; Judy Chicago and Mary Ross Taylor, Through the Flower, Benicia, California; Andrew Blanks, Jr., art teacher, Johnston Middle School, Houston; Barbara Pearson Roberts, teacher, Sabal Palm Elementary School, Tallahassee; Shirley and Terry McManus, puppetry consultants, "Puppets Please," San Diego; Dr. Wayne Woodward, associate professor of art education, Georgia Southwestern College; Mary Riggs of Riggs Galleries, San Diego; Anna Ganahl, Director of Public Relations, Art Center College of Design, Pasadena; Françoise Gilot, artist, La Jolla, California; Leven C. Leatherbury, independent consultant in art education, San Diego; Betty Cavanaugh, curriculum consultant in art education, Upland, California; Joel Hagen, artist and writer, Oakdale, California; Kellene Champlin, Art Supervisor, Fulton County Schools, Atlanta; Mar Gwen Land, art teacher, Montgomery Jr. High School, San Diego; LaRene McGregor, fiber artist, McKenzie Bridge, Oregon; Norma Wilson, former art teacher and editorial advisor, San Diego; Dr. Ann S. Richardson, Supervisor of Art, Foreign Languages, and Gifted and Talented Education, Charles County Public Schools, LaPlata, Maryland; Talli Larrick, educator and writer, El Cajon, California; Mary Apuli, Coordinator of Elementary Program, Indiana School District No. 16, Minneapolis; Carol Widdop-Sonka, artist and writer, San Diego; Virginia Fitzpatrick, art educator and writer, Bloomington, Indiana; Evelyn Ackerman, artist, Era Industries, Culver City, California; Judy Kugel, teacher trainer for Learning to Read Through the Arts, New York City; Arlie Zolynas, educator and author, San Diego; Nancy Remington, Principal, Sacramento Country Day School, Sacramento; Kay Alexander, Art Consultant, Palo Alto School District, Palo Alto, California; Billie Phillips, Lead Art Supervisor, St. Louis Public Schools, St. Louis; Sister Marie Albert, S.S.J., Principal, St. Callistus School, Philadelphia; Robert Vickrey, artist, Orleans, Massachusetts.

Although it is impossible to acknowledge all the contributors to this project, we express special thanks for the generous efforts of the following individuals: Janet Reim, Gail Kozar, Rae Murphy, Jan Thompson, Gerald Williams, Timothy Asfazadour, Judy Cannon, Helen Negley, Crystal Thorson, Rachelle and Tyler Bruford, Mary Bluhm, David Zielinski, David Oliver, Daniel and Carl Bohman, Anne G. Allen, Bao Vuong, Gail W. Guth, Signe Ringbloom, Claire Murphy, Joan Blaine, Patrice M. Sparks, and Larke Johnston.

Coronado Staff: Marsha Barrett Lippincott, Level One Editor; Janet Kylstad Coulon, Level Two Editor; Deanne Kells Cordell, Level Three Editor; Carol Spirkoff Prime, Level Four Editor; Patricia McCambridge, Level Five Editor; DeLynn Decker, Level Six Editor; Janis Heppell, Project Designer; Lisa Peters, Designer; Myrtali Anagnostopoulos, Designer; Debra Saleny, Photo Research.